Physical Characteristics of the Akita

(from the American Kennel Club breed standard)

Tail: Large and full, set high and carried over back or against flank in a three-quarter, full, or double curl, always dipping to or below level of back. Root large and strong. Hair coarse, straight and full, with no appearance of a plume.

Body: Longer than high, as 10 is to 9 in males; 11 to 9 in bitches. Chest wide and deep; depth of chest is one-half height of dog at shoulder. Ribs well sprung, brisket well developed. Level back with firmly-muscled loin and moderate tuck-up. Skin pliant but not loose.

Coat: Double-coated. Undercoat thick, soft, dense and shorter than outer coat. Outer coat straight, harsh and standing somewhat off body.

Hindquarters: Width, muscular development and bone comparable to forequarters. Upper thighs well developed. Stifle moderately bent and hocks well let down, turning neither in nor out.

Size: Males 26 to 28 inches at the withers; bitches 24 to 26 inches.

Dewclaws: On front legs generally not removed; dewclaws on hind legs generally removed.

Feet: Cat feet, well knuckled up with thick pads. Feet straight ahead.

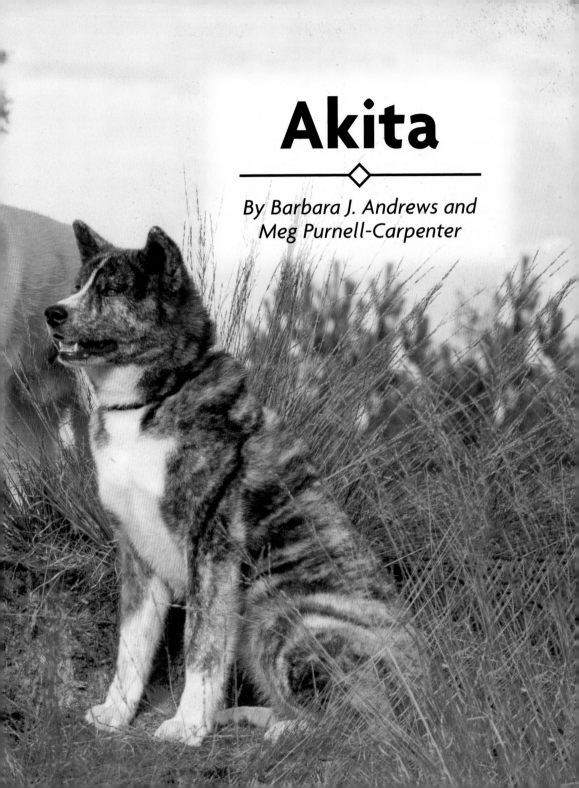

Akita

By Barbara J. Andrews and
Meg Purnell-Carpenter

Contents

KENNEL CLUB BOOKS: **AKITA**
ISBN: 1-59378-298-5

Photographs by Carol Ann Johnson
with additional photos by Norvia Behling, T.J. Calhoun, Carolina Biological Supply, Doskocil, Isabelle Français, James Hayden-Yoav, James R. Hayden, RBP, Bill Jonas, Dwight R. Kuhn, Dr. Dennis Kunkel, Mikki Pet Products, Phototake, Jean Claude Revy, Dr. Andrew Spielman, and Alice van Kempen.

The publisher wishes to thank Bill and B.J. Andrews, Marc Blanc, Steve and Judy Bolding, C.T. & N. Calloway, M. Fisk, Maurizio Moretto, Elaine Nussbaum, Paladin Kennels, Meg Purnell-Carpenter, Donald See, M. White Jr. and the rest of the owners for allowing their dogs to be photographed for this book.

Illustrations by Patricia Peters

The Akita was a known dog as early as 500 BC. It appeared as a distinct type in written records more than 300 years ago. One peek at a litter of Akita puppies and the world's fascination with this ancient Japanese breed becomes evident.

ORIGINS OF THE AKITA OF JAPAN

As is so with many of the old wolf-spitz breeds, the origin of the Akita is a puzzle. Drawings and other artifacts dating back more than 3,000 years document the existence of a wolf-spitz dog throughout Asia. This early domesticated dog evolved into the breeds that we now call the Chow Chow, Norwegian Elkhound, husky (generic term) and, quite likely, the Akita. Actually, the Akita's remote ancestors became identifiable by about 500 BC, and we can trace the Akita-inu as a distinct type back through over 300 years of written records.

The ancestors of the Akita may even have come to Japan before the European continent was separated by the Sea of Japan. Such ancient dogs were excellent bear hunters and served man in many ways. Dogs with big, double- or triple-layered, weather-resistant coats are usually referred to as Arctic-type dogs and have always had a history of working for their keep. The Akita might be said to fit into that category as well. It is a very complex breed and, like a colorful painting that has been converted into an intricate jigsaw puzzle, there are hundreds of pieces which, when fitted properly, become the masterpiece we call the Akita.

To further complicate accurate research, the Akita's beginnings are obscured by a very old culture that is in itself still a mystery to most of the rest of the world. There is so much that we do not understand but that made perfectly good sense to the Japanese dog lover of the last century. For example, we are positively squeamish about skinning one of our beloved dogs, but the Japanese did so with the dogs they most revered. The skins were tanned and thus the favorite dog was preserved. The famous companion Akita, Hachi-Ko, is not only remembered as an awe-inspiring statue but also was preserved and is on display in one of Japan's national museums.

The Akita's importance in the daily life of the Japanese family is obvious in that he is considered a symbol of health and prosperity. In most countries, one presents a new mother or sick friend with flowers. In Japan, an Akita is still given as a token of the bearer's wishes for a speedy recovery and all things good.

We are enchanted by Oriental customs related to the Akita, but we do indeed find it difficult to understand why dogs are still eaten in many Asian countries or why the Japanese were once so fond of appalling sporting events involving dogs. Although dogs have been and are still perceived as food in other parts of the world, it is a puzzling contradiction in Japan, where the Akita has long been so highly regarded. Equally puzzling, long ago it was considered entertaining to turn a hundred dogs loose in an arena as targets for men with bows and arrows. Thankfully, this is no longer done.

Along the same lines, dog fighting is another inhumane practise that once thrived in Japan. Probably as old as is the semi-domesticated canine, it has also been practiced in many other countries, including Britain and the US. The pastime of pitting dogs against one another evolved in Japan during the Kamakura period (1185–1333) under the reign of Shogun Hojo Takatoki. The Satake Clan of Odate City (a.k.a. "Dog Fighting Capital") crossed the Akita-Matagi-inu with the mastiff-like Tosa-inu for precisely that purpose. During the relatively recent Meiji period

THE EMPEROR'S DOGSPEAK

Akitas were once owned only by royalty and a special language was used to talk to them.

(1866–1912), the Enyukai Club, formed in Odate in 1897, was still in vogue. Several such clubs hosted fighting tournaments, where eager fans would gather for a full day of entertainment. In 1908 Japan passed ordinances that officially outlawed the fighting of dogs. Shocking as that may be, it is in stark contrast to the fact that it wasn't until the 1980s that the US officially forbid dog fighting in every state and began to prosecute offenders.

The Akita is still a dominant dog, but thankfully the influence of the Tosa and other such fighting breeds has waned and the Akita is rarely quarrelsome. Very sure of his superiority over other dogs, he is quite the gentleman and can be surprisingly tolerant.

Despite the rather sketchy history of the Akita in Japan, we know he served a variety of useful purposes at different levels of society. As the peasant's dog, he was a hunter. As the sporting partner of royalty, he is said to have hunted with falcons. Although he is reputed to have been a good water retriever, we personally refute that as we've never known an adult Akita to swim without strong encouragement! Wade? Lay down in cool water? Of course. Swim for the fun of it or to retrieve anything? Never.

As a hunter of big game such as mountain bear and boar, he was (and in parts of America, still is)

The Japanese have been recording tales about Akitas for hundreds of years. This statue, in bronze, commemorates the legendary loyal Akita Hachi-Ko.

quite adept. His courage is well documented and his fighting ability is legendary. Although he does not "give tongue," as do the hound breeds, hunters will be able to follow the direction of the chase as the mighty bear and even the wild boar will not run as far as other game. They will be brought to bay by the dogs, and the tenacity and courage of the Akita will hold the quarry until the hunters arrive.

Written history tells us that the breed at one time was officially owned only by the Japanese ruling class. In fact, during Emperor Senka's reign, the office of Dog Keeper was officially established. There was even a special language used when talking to or about an Akita; the words them-

WHAT IS THE REGISTER OF MERIT?

The suffix ROM (Register of Merit) indicates that an Akita has produced in the top 2 to 3% of breeding animals, a sure indicator of genetic superiority. The suffix was initiated in the early 1970s by author B.J. Andrews in her widely acclaimed *Akita Handbook.* Her record-keeping and publications were later adopted by the Akita Club of America. Two other suffixes are used: ROMX and ROMP, which can be combined as ROMXP. The "X" indicates that the dog has produced twice the number of progeny required for the ROM. The "P" indicates that the dog has produced an ROM-holding progeny.

The O'BJ dogs of the Andrews' breeding in America claim the top three positions for the sires, namely Ch. Okii Yubi's Sachmo of Makoto, ROMXP, who produced 101 champions, 16 of whom hold ROMs; Ch. The Widow-Maker O'BJ, ROMXP, who produced 65 champions, 3 of whom hold ROMs; and Ch. O'BJ Bigson of Sachmo, ROMXP, who produced 49 champions, 3 of whom hold ROMs. The top dam of all time is Ch. The Mad Hatter O'BJ, ROMXP, who produced 16 champions, 2 of whom have also produced ROM holders.

used to denote rank and there were very specific ways in which the leash could be used to tie up an Akita. Special dogs achieved greater rank according to their degree of training and, of course, the personal preference of the Emperor.

The Akita, like many breeds, derived its name from the area with which it was most closely associated. The Akita's primary development is associated with Akita Prefecture in the northern part of Japan, Honshu Island. More specifically, the breed is closely connected to a particular town in Akita Prefecture called Odate City, also known as "Dog City" and "Boulevard of Dogs." Mr. Shigiei Izumi, the mayor of Odate City, founded the Akita Dog Preservation Society in 1926.

As a point of clarification, one should not be confused by Japanese dog terms such as "ken" and "inu." These words are used as a suffix, attached by a hyphen, as in Akita-ken or Shiba-inu. Both simply mean "dog."

Japan established Natural (not "National" as it is sometimes mistakenly printed) Monument legislation during the middle of the Taisho era (1912–1926). This was designed to preserve culturally significant objects, including animals. In the early part of the Showa era, about 1925, Katsusuke Ishihara bemoaned the fact that there were very few dogs that

selves were actually called "dog words." The care and training of an Akita were very ritualized. There were also special leashes

possessed what he considered to be the standard in each breed. So it was with the Akita. Dr. Watase, who pioneered the Natural Monument bill, was most disappointed when he journeyed to Odate to study the Akita-inu.

Odate City was a logical place from which to begin his search as it was, at that time in history, a very remote area surrounded by towering mountain ranges and shut off to winter travel by severe weather. The local dog that was to become the Akita-inu evolved for several hundred years, untouched by other developing breed types. The large region that includes Akita Prefecture remained quite isolated until the 14th century. As a point of fact, the Hokkaido region is often referred to as the Ezo-chi or "Land of the Ainus" even today.

Dogs from China and Korea had begun to trickle into Japan under the reign of Emperor Jinmu, about 660 BC. With the introduction of Christianity in the 15th century, all sorts of dogs began to arrive in Japan along with their European owners. The mastiff-type influence is still seen in dogs with an excess of skin, loose eyelids and hanging ears. The Elkhound and Keeshond-type dogs also left their marks on the native dog that the world would one day know as the Akita. The pinto coloration, particularly black and white, may have been

The Karelian Bear Dog shares its black and white pattern and ability to tackle a bear with the Akita.

from the non-spitz type Chinese Karainu. Scrolls from the early Kamakura era (1185–1249) also depict pinto dogs of Akita type as part of the background. Photographs of the early 1900s include black pinto Akitas.

As an aside, there now exists a breed, the Karelian Bear Dog, that is undeniably similar to a black and white Akita. The breed closely resembles the lesser known Russo-European Laika, which descends from Russian and Finnish dogs from the area once known as Karelia. It is said to be equally as fierce and courageous as the Akita. The breed has been recognized by the Canadian Kennel Club for many years and has a devoted following in that country. One must wonder if the

NATIVE SPITZ BREEDS OF JAPAN

BREED: **Hokkaido/Ainu**

SIZE: 18-22 in (46-56 cms)
COLORS: Red
UTILITY: Bear/deer hunting/guarding

BREED: **Shiba-inu**

SIZE: 14.5–15.5 in (37-39 cms)
COLORS: Red, red sesame, black and tan
UTILITY: Small bird hunting/companion

BREED: **Shikoku**

SIZE: 17–22 in (43-56 cms)
COLORS: White, fawn, tan gray, pied
UTILITY: Deer hunting/companion

BREED: **Kai**

SIZE: 18-23.5 in (46-60 cms)
COLORS: Brindle
UTILITY: Deer Hunting

BREED: **Kishu**
SIZE: 17-22 in (43-56 cms)
COLORS: White
UTILITY: Herding/guarding

BREED: **Akita**

SIZE: 24-28 in (61-71 cms)
COLORS: Any including brindle or pinto
UTILITY: Bear/boar hunting/guarding

genes have somehow mingled with Canadian husky-type dogs. The Karelian is indeed a handsome dog, though of smaller stature than today's Akita.

Regrettably, Dr. Watase found no dogs representative of a Natural Monument in what should have been the epicenter, the city of Odate. We surmise that he was searching for a dog once known as the Matagi-inu, a word meaning "hunter." The native red dog with a light-colored muzzle, similar in coloration and type to primitive canines all over the world, had become diluted by the European dogs and the inevitable crossbreeding that resulted. Thus began a concerted effort to restore the type and color that were considered "pure."

The primitive color pattern was strengthened during the resurgence of interest that occurred in the late 1980s. It is now considered representative of the Japanese Akita, as is white and brindle coloration and the absence of a black muzzle. The older generation Japanese visibly shudder at black dogs with white boots and vest—color patterns said to be representative of traditional funeral attire. None of this really matters to us because pintos, black masks and even "formally dressed" black dogs with white markings afford us with an infinite palette from which to choose a beautiful Akita.

TEN BREEDS OF JAPAN

The six Japanese spitz breeds are divided by size, namely the Akita as the large breed; the Shiba as the small breed, and four medium-size breeds, Kai, Kishu, Shikoku and Hokkaido (or Ainu). Only the Akita and Shiba have established significant followings outside Japan. There are four other recognized Japanese breeds, including the giant mastiff breed known as the Tosa, the lovely toy breed known as the Chin, the solid white Japanese Spitz and the diminutive Japanese Terrier. Of course, the Chin is the most popular of these breeds worldwide. In Japan, the Shiba is the most popular Japanese breed, followed by the Japanese Spitz, Chin and Akita.

American dog author and good friend to both authors, Andrew De Prisco with his two prized Japanese Shiba-inu companions and show dogs.

In 1927 the Akiho (Akita-inu Hozankai Society) was established in Odate City. Nippo (Nippo-ken Hozankai) followed in 1928 and

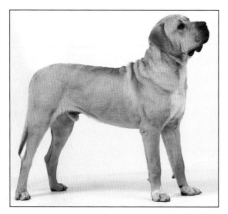

The Tosa-inu stands 24.5-28 in (62-71 cms) and can weigh up to 200 lb (90 kgs).

the Akita-inu Akikyo in 1948, each organization determined to restore the Akita as a Natural Monument and each was, in its way, quite successful in doing so.

THE AKITA GOES TO AMERICA

A powerful influence in restoring the Akita to the rest of the world occurred when soldiers returning to the US in the late 1940s smuggled the big dogs out of Japan. These "Akitas" were not selected due to any concern for type, but because of their appeal as individual dogs. Members of America's fighting forces must have been very drawn to the courage and loyalty of the dogs known as Akitas. As there were so few dogs brought back to the United States at that time, there was only the rarest opportunity to breed an Akita to an Akita. A prominent American family later thought it worthwhile to import some dogs, albeit purchased at pet shops, from the Tokyo area. Some were

probably pure-bred, some were relatively healthy, but some failed in both regards. A couple of those dogs became strong genetic influences during the early years in the US, and many breeders in America believe that may in part account for the lack of consistent type and for the serious inbred genetic defects found in the breed.

In 1955 the Akita moved into the American Kennel Club's (AKC) Miscellaneous Class, a class similar to the Import Class in the UK, where new breeds can be exhibited. In 1956 what was eventually to become the American Akita Club was forming, and it came into formal existence in 1959. Americans had spent many years in the formation of various clubs, with individual owners struggling to become the dominant authority on Akitas. It has been said that most Akita people exhibit the same bold and dominant traits as their dogs! The splinter clubs and disagreements were resolved by the end of 1972, at which time the AKC approved the Akita Club of America's breed standard.

Japanese imports could, however, still be registered as foundation stock until February 1974. The American gene pool, which established the type known worldwide as the "American Akita," was indeed rather small in comparison to those of many other well-established breeds.

Original foundation stock consisted of little more than 100 distinct pedigrees.

It must be noted, however, that those original pedigrees were so questionable as to be considered mongrelized. Many of the original dogs brought back from Japan were not of pure parentage; therefore, a narrow gene pool was hardly the case. Dogs that had survived the worst of the war were in fact left to wander the streets by owners who loved them too much to destroy them. They could not risk being identified as owners of such large dogs, whose voracious appetites further reduced the scarce food supply, so they abandoned the dogs to the streets to fend for themselves.

As indicated by numerous photos of the time, Nature took her course and the Akita interbred with mongrels and strays of other breeds. Indeed, Helen Keller's Akita, with whom she was frequently photographed, would not today be regarded as pure-bred in either America or Japan. Nonetheless, those early imports had the intelligence and character that make the breed so remarkable and unique today.

Having arrived in America, the breed that would later be

A pinto Akita on the move. Coloration doesn't matter—movement, temperament and soundness are all!

Author B.J. Andrews with Ch. O'BJ Nikki No Takara, moving in the ring at the American National Specialty, where she won first in the American-bred Class over 20 bitches. Nikki is an inbred daughter of the great Sachmo, considered by most experts to be the best Akita ever bred.

Sire of over 100 American champions, this is the one and only Ch. Okii Yubi's Sachmo of Makoto, owned by Bill and B.J. Andrews. He is the number-one sire of all Working breeds in the US.

Ch. O'BJ BigSon of Sachmo was the number-three sire of all time, photographed at the modest age of eleven. He sired 48 American champions, including tens of specialty winners and ROM get.

registered as the Akita was further out-crossed by random matings. In addition, there continued to be a few dogs imported from Japan. We must apply common sense rather than rhetoric in order to establish a factual genetic basis of the breed in America. Japan was busy reconstructing itself and any sort of cash income was most welcome; therefore, little attention was paid to the purity of dogs sold on the street or in pet shops. With the stud book so lacking in authenticity, the progeny of those matings subsequently, and as a matter of course, became AKC-registered.

There were, fortunately, a handful of dominant dogs that led to the development of several prominent lines. Issei Riki Oji Go was bred to Kuma's Akai Kosho-Go, and that mating produced Ch.

Mitsu Kuma's O Kashihime-Go, Mitsu Kuma's Splashdown (US top sire Sachmo's granddam) and the breed's first Group winner, Ch. Mitsu Kuma's Tora Oji Go, owned by Terry Wright. The Mullens' Mitsu Kuma kennels in New Jersey became well known for its contributions to the early development of the Akita in the States.

The Frerose Kennels of Fred Duane was founded on top show dog and producer, Am-Can-Berm. Ch. Kenjiko Royal Tenji, ROMXP. Jojo, as he was called, is the grandson of Japanese import Teddy Bear of Toyohashi Seiko.

A handsome import, Gyokushu of Tojo Kensha was the grandsire of Krug's Sotto and Michiko of Kensha. Santo became a foundation sire for Bettye and Francis Krug of Maryland, and Michiko was a top producer for

the Sakura kennels of Barbara Miller. Ch. Krug's Ichiban Akemi-Go was the top-winning Akita bitch prior to AKC recognition.

A small kennel was established by Bob Campbell, who shipped one of his foundation bitches, Namesu-Joo, back to the West Coast to be bred to the mighty Ashibaya Kuma, owned by Bea Hunt. That mating produced Yukan No Okii Yubi, ROMP, who sired Ch. Okii Yubi's Dragon House Ko-Go, ROMXP, owned by Bill and Barbara Andrews. Ko-Go went on to become the number-two all-time top-producing dam. Bob Campbell is credited with having bred many top producers, including the number-one sire of all Working Group dogs in the US, Ch. Okii Yubi's Sachmo of Makoto, ROMXP. Sachmo, as he was called, was also owned by Bill and Barbara (B.J.) Andrews. Sachmo's grandsire was California's top winner and producer, Ch. Fukumoto's Ashibaya Kuma, a grandson of Jap. Gr. Ch. Kinsho-Go, the son of Mexican Ch. Triple K Hayai Taka.

The dominant brindle bitch, Jap. Gr. Ch. Haru Hime, produced very well for Barbara Confer when bred to Jap. Gr. Ch. Teddy Bear of Toyohashi Seiko. Ch. Sakusaku's Tom Cat-Go, ROMP, is just one of the many top winners and Register of Merit progeny produced by Teddy Bear and Haru Hime.

Eng. Ch. Paper Doll O'BJ, sired by BigSon, was a lovely Akita, photographed at ten years of age. She was owned by C. and N. Callaway.

Walter Kam brought several Akitas from Japan to found Triple K kennels, in San Gabriel, California. They produced such great dogs as Mex. Ch. Triple K Hayai Taka and Ch. Triple K Shinya Ningyo, who produced Triple K Miko, the mother of the aforementioned Ashibaya Kuma. Shina Ningyo was herself a daughter of Jap. Gr. Ch. Kinsho-Go, a son of Jap. Gr. Ch. Kinsho-Go Abe.

The Akita Tani kennel of Liz Harrel was founded on two great dogs that traced directly to the Kams' original import stock. Akita Tani's Shoyo-Go was sired by Jap. Gr. Ch. Kinsho-Go, who was also the sire of Shinya Ningyo. Shoyo-Go was successfully bred to two of his half-sisters by Kinsho-Go, and also back to his dam, Kokoro. As he was already the product of a father-daughter breeding, the litter produced the very inbred dog Akita Tani's Tatsumaki, ROM.

Barbara and Mac McDougle, of the kennel name Gin Gin, bred a dog destined to become one of first top winners when the breed was finally recognized—Can-Mex-CACIB Ch. Gin Gin Haiyaku-Go of Saku Saku. Chester, as he was known, was sired by Tom Cat, and, although he became sterile at an early age, he was a top show dog.

The famous Ch. Okii Yubi's Sachmo of Makoto, ROMXP, blended foundation lines from both coasts through his sire, Mikado No Kin Hozan, ROMP, and his dam, Mariko No Kin Hozan. Sachmo was purchased by Bill and Barbara Andrews as an eight-week-old puppy. Although they had studied pedigrees and were far from new to the sport, the Andrews admit that neither they nor Bob Campbell, Sachmo's breeder, had any inkling of what lie ahead.

Sachmo became the sire of 101 AKC champions and is credited with having set a consistency of type that has yet to be equaled. He was dominant for his full off-standing coat, tight features with no wrinkles, a huge bear-like head with small eyes and ears and, despite heavy round bone, the muscular body of a true athlete. He also possessed the courage of the old bear dogs of Japan, combined with the staunch protectiveness typical of the later molosser breeds' influence. To people the world over, he and many of his O'BJ-bred descendants typified the "American Akita."

On the genetic strength of Sachmo and Ko-Go, both of whom were astute purchases from Bob Campbell, the Andrews quickly became the top Akita kennel in the Western world. With only three to six bitches, the Andrews produced more champions, Registers of Merit and top winners than any other two kennels combined.

The famous Ch. The Widow-Maker O'BJ was linebred on Sachmo, and he quickly became the top-winning Akita of all time. With his carefully constructed pedigree and the few selective matings that the Andrews arranged, The Widow-Maker surpassed Ch. O'BJ BigSon of Sachmo, also bred and owned by Bill and BJ Andrews, as the number-two breed sire. The three top sires of all time remain: Sachmo with 101 champions, Widow-Maker with 78 champions, and BigSon with 49 champions.

The Akita is one of only a very few AKC-registered breeds that allows all colors, even though this clearly shows the diversity of a hybridized background. In Japan, they are not as enthralled by outward evidence of genetic "impurity," and many of the

colors that were highly favored in Japan are now forbidden, though they are still allowed in America and on the Continent.

From the 1960s to the 1980s, the breed continued to develop and became ever more popular in the US, spreading to Canada, Mexico and even South America. All colors were welcomed as long as the dog was large and impressive and had a "big bear head." Few gave thought to what was going on in Japan, although some American breeders were careful not to lose the short thick ears and the dense thick coats so typical of "Northern" dogs. Tails began to loosen as some American lines forfeited the dominant character in favor of the softer temperament, which inevitably leads to "lazy" tails. A dominant canine, whether wolf or domestic, is always identified by his high tail carriage. A submissive dog approaches another dog or a person with flattened ears and a low or tucked tail. While some American breeders such as the Andrews worked hard to maintain the Japanese features, such as tight skin and tails, big coats, small ears, etc., many lines drifted a bit toward the German Shepherd Dog or mastiff influence.

As some of the original imports that reflected the mastiff and other European-breed influences were rather short coated, the US became divided on the matter of coat length. While some coats were indeed too long (often called "long coats"), many were inarguably too short! Freckles began to appear along with shorter and softer textured coats. Attempts were made to correct these type faults, but it was diffi-cult to maintain "Japanese" type in the large strong working-dog type that had become so popular in the Western world.

THE GREAT AKITA DEBATE

History of the breed in the Western world has to begin with the US and, unfortunately, it has to include the great debate that erupted there. All importation (to be registered) to America was cut off from 1974 until April 1992, when the American Kennel Club (AKC) finally recognized the Japanese Kennel Club (JKC) and its stud book. One reason that the AKC steadfastly refused to honor Japanese export pedigrees was the concern for the authenticity of the paperwork and the purity of breeds. This was considered by many to be a bit hypocritical, as during that time span, the AKC busily accepted several breeds known to have been hybrids of existent types in various coun-tries. Prior to importation of the African jungle Basenji in the 1980s, the AKC approved the Dalmatian-to-Pointer breedings in order to correct a genetic health defect in the spotted breed.

Suddenly, the AKC recognized the JKC stud book. The AKC had slipped up when it accepted the Japanese Kennel Club records on behalf of Japanese Shibas, which were, in fact, all recent Japanese imports. Traditionalists as well as those Akita breeders who were looking for something "new and different" latched on to the oppor-tunity to once again import Akitas from Japan.

Then, more than 25 years after first seeking AKC recognition, in efforts to circumvent having to go through the same lengthy steps of meeting registration requirements, a small faction of enterprising Akita owners in the US cited the small number of "pedigrees" represented by early AKC enroll-ment figures. They said that by the late 1990s the breed was in need of new genes because of the small number of early pedigrees and, therefore, the imports must be registered as Akitas, all one breed, so as to allow interbreed-ing. To most Americans, that made as much sense as breeding Shibas to Akitas to increase genetic diversity.

The big debate on "the split" was thus born. Those persons still active in the breed who were knowledgeable of the factual history of the breed in America knew that the beginnings of the breed were quite random. One has only to look at photos of early Akitas in the United States to acknowledge that the breed had the stamp of many breeds. They watched incredulously as new dogs came in from Japan and were bred to American Akitas. Everyone agreed that some of imported dogs were incredibly

At a show in Chile, Grandson to The Widow-Maker O'BJ, South American Ch. Seisan's Ultimate Warrior, known as Spike, won the Group and was ranked fourth in the show.

beautiful, but all agreed that they were totally different than those in America. And so began the quandary and the debate over "one breed or two" that earned the Akita the dubious distinction of becoming "the breed with the most names."

Just as fanciers in Japan worked diligently to restore the Akita there to what was believed to be its original form, American breeders worked for 30 years to create uniformity and genetic knowledge of the breed. Bitterness prevails between breeders in the US and elsewhere.

Even the co-authors of this book are in disagreement. Mrs. Barbara Andrews is in favor of keeping the two breeds "separate but equal," as is currently the case in most countries. Mrs. Meg Purnell-Carpenter of the UK, having had early access to a very good Japanese dog and being one of the first to pioneer the crossing of American bloodlines with

The perfect "Blend": Overhill's Pacer, bred by author Meg Purnell-Carpenter's out of her American import, from author BJ Andrews, O'BJ White Hope of Overhill.

Japanese lines, believes it can be good for the breed to take advantage of both genetic pools.

Meg explains thusly, "I find it very sad that the Akitas are to be divided into two breeds, especially when, according to the standards, color is the only dividing difference between the two. I sincerely hope this does not happen in the UK; I very much hope we could stay as we are. At present we are able—if we wish—to exhibit both types, also to breed the two together. If we maintain our present system, we could possibly improve the overall qual-

ity of the breed. We would also have a much wider gene pool than other countries that could become very restricted if they cannot mix the two types. Both types have a lot to offer; both also have their faults. With careful selective breeding, combining the two together, I feel that we in the UK would have the advantage over the other countries. I have to say I would heartily support keeping our standard open, as it is now."

Many Americans consider it ironic that Japan's breeders succeeded so well in re-establishing what they consider to be the native type whereas Americans have dissolved ten generations of dedicated work by their predecessors through engaging in the cross-breeding of the late 1990s. Because the progeny of such matings is neither American nor Japanese, they are commonly called "Tweenies," meaning betwixt and between. Those Americans who went to considerable trouble and expense to import top-quality and top-winning Japanese dogs are as disappointed to see the many generations of pure Japanese breeding destroyed as are the Japanese breeders themselves. Tweenie breeders have begun a movement to change the term to "Blends," as it is considered more acceptable, but most Americans are firmly of the opinion that a mongrel is a mongrel, no matter how beautiful both parents were! That conviction led to the formation of the Japanese Akita Club of America, a club recognized by Japan and one that advocates only the breeding of pure Japanese stock with no American Akita influence.

Adding fuel to the growing controversy of the 1990s, in 1999 at a meeting at the World Dog Show, the General Assembly approved the division of the breed, and the new FCI breed standards were accepted. Henceforth, in all FCI countries the Akita breed has been split to become known as the Japanese Akita and the Great Japanese Dog, formerly the American Akita.

To further complicate life for those who consider the Akita as a spitz-type working-guarding dog, the General Assembly assigned the Great Japanese Dog to Group Two in all FCI countries. That group contains breeds such as the Pinschers, Schnauzers, Molossians and the Swiss Mountain and Cattle Dogs. The Japanese Akita remains in Group Five, rightly so, with the Spitz and Primitive Dogs.

Americans were not at all happy with the designation and, in fact, the breed is still known as before as the Japanese Akita and the American Akita. In fact, in an unconscious attempt to maintain sanity, the defining terms "Japanese" and "American" are in even more common usage. To the confusion of all, the Akita is in the unique position of having more than four different "official" breed standards throughout the world!

Physical appearance and behavioral characteristics of the two pure strains remain quite different. The American Akita largely predominates in the Western world and is exemplified by large bone, greater overall size and a spectacular array of colors and markings. The Japanese sought to re-establish the type native to their country and

The American Akita authority, Mr. Rayne with his wife, presenting the trophy to a winner in the UK.

the other and those who wish the foreign dogs would all go away! As it was diversity of color, size and idealism that were the basis for attraction to this marvelous breed in America, some devotees merely smile as they realize that nothing has changed.

THE AKITA IN THE UNITED KINGDOM

Throughout the 1970s and 1980s, the Akita firmly established itself in the US, becoming widely popular, with several taking top awards on the show scene. Mrs. Andrews sent a pair of youngsters to Australia via the Overhill quarantine kennels of Mrs. Meg Purnell-Carpenter in the UK. In the course of so doing, Mrs. Purnell-Carpenter, a very prominent breeder of working German Shepherds, fell in love with the Akita during what was then a full year's quarantine at her kennel near Bristol.

Knowing dogs so well, Mrs. Purnell-Carpenter began to look at the breed, some of which had already arrived in the UK. The first to arrive had been a fawn and white bitch from Canada, imported in 1980 by Marion Sergeant. She was Davos Wata Kyshi Tomo-Dachi of Tegwani, affectionately known as Tania. Marion did much winning with her in the early days of the Akita in the UK.

The first male to arrive in the UK was Kosho Ki's Kai of Lindrick

strongly seek a dog with decisively Oriental features and very limited colors. This has resulted in a wide gap between the best of the lighter boned, smaller, lushly coated, exquisitely beautiful Japanese dogs and the substantially larger, stronger, heavier proportioned and shorter coated American Akitas.

Having entered the new millennium, the world-wide Akita fancy seems unhappily divided into three factions: those who would keep the American and Japanese types separate, those who feel that each type could benefit from blending certain virtues of

and Tegwani. His dam was an American and Canadian champion, and he was imported in partnership by Mike and Joyce Window with Kath and Gerald Mitchell. Another import to arrive about this time was the bitch Yikihime Go, imported by Mrs. Beryl Mason from Japan. These original imports were followed very swiftly by several others, all from America with but one exception.

Mrs. Purnell-Carpenter decided it was time to go full out and bring in a top bloodline from America. Having become acquainted with Mrs. Andrews through caring for the two pups in quarantine, she inquired for an O'BJ dog. The result was a magnificent white bitch sired by the then top-winning male in America, the Andrews' Ch. Kakwa's Orca. O'BJ White Hope at Overhill charmed all who met her and was soon followed by the first American champion to come into the UK.

Ch. Sachette No Okii Yubi was sent to England by Mrs. Andrews, who maintained that she and the Sachmo daughter had a "thing" going whereby Sachette laid awake at night thinking of ways to thwart her owner's plans! Had it not been for Mrs. Andrews' laughing annoyance with Sachette, a bitch of such spectacular quality might never have been allowed to leave America.

Sachette was the dam of the first litter to be born in the UK.

She whelped a lovely litter sired by O'BJ Aces High on October 23, 1983. Aces was a dog completing his residency in quarantine before traveling on to Australia, where he became a successful sire as well. Very quickly there were several other litters born in the UK, including a Japanese-bred litter. These first puppies helped to firmly establish the breed in England.

In those early days, the Akita in the UK had to compete in the Any Variety Not Separately Classified (AVNSC) Classes, being one of the last breeds to come into the country without having to go onto the import register. The AVNSC competitors in other breeds quickly became

Ten-time Best-in-Show winner, Ch. The Widow-Maker O'BJ is the number-two sire of all time, having 78 American champion get to his fame. This great dog had thousands of fans on both sides of the pond.

aware that the Akita was here to stay, constantly beating them in hot competition to take top honors under not only the English judges but also others experienced in the breed from abroad who appreciated their presence and qualities.

In a very short time, it became noticeable that the AVNSC Class looked like "the Akita Class," with 90% being filled with that breed. Competitors in other AVNSC breeds were relieved when Akitas were given their own classification.

At the 1985 Crufts Dog Show, Mrs. Andrews handled Overhill's Lizzys Girl to Best of Breed AVNSC, the first Akita and the first American to win this top honor. It was especially exciting for these co-authors, as Lizzys Girl was from the first litter born in the UK, out of the first imported American champion, the bitch sent to the UK by Mrs. Andrews! Lizzy and her sisters, Overhill's Marlows Miracle and Overhill's Kita Mori, were out of extremely successful show dogs and producers.

As in the US, at the beginning there was a great division over the establishment of a breed club. Eventually four people, two representatives from each side, called a meeting of all Akita enthusiasts. The four were John Dunhill, Jill Bingham, Mike Window and Meg Purnell-Carpenter, who together formed the Japanese Akita Association, which gained acceptance by The Kennel Club in 1987.

The Japanese Akita, as the breed is known in the UK, competes in the Utility Group, whereas in the US the breed competes in the Working Group. October 1998 saw the first Japanese Akita Association Open Show, run by the newly formed breed club, and the first Challenge Certificates (CCs) were awarded at Crufts in 1990. The dog CC and Best of Breed went to the imported Ch. Tamarlane's Veni Vidi Vici, owned by Mike Window. Veni Vidi Vici went on to become the first male champion to be made up; the first bitch was Ch. Goshens Classy Sassy at Redwitch, owned by Dave and Jenny Killilea.

Since those early days, the breed has progressed, not only in the show ring but also in other areas. There are many Akitas that have received The Kennel Club Good Citizen Award. Some have become therapy dogs while others have taken to sledding. There is even one that has been participating in Afghan racing and has qualified in acceptable times!

The English American-type Akitas have made a great impact world-wide, many taking Best in Show and other top awards. In the UK, the Akitas have consistently been winning groups and group placements at Championship Shows, which must make this

breed one of the most competitive in the show world.

In a published interview wherein she was asked which Akita not owned or bred at Overhill she considered to be the closest to the standard, Mrs. Purnell-Carpenter responded thusly, "The Akita closest to the breed standard would be The Widow Maker O'BJ. This superb male—a top-winning Akita in the US—is full of breed type, the nearest example to the breed standard. His outstanding attributes for me would be his wonderful head, hindquarter, vibrant color, movement and overall balance. I set him as my ideal. The Akita I have personally owned and bred that has been nearest to my ideal would be my Ch. Overhill's Cherokee Lite Fut, a daughter of the above dog. She inherited her sire's outstanding movement and hindquarters, excelling in bone and substance. She was one of the early English champion bitches to gain her title. In my opinion she would compete very strongly in today's competition."

Breeders in the UK have been surprisingly successful in restoring and selecting for correct ear size and tail carriage, and, in the 21st century, two of the topwinning Great Japanese Dogs in Europe are American imports owned by Katharina Round in France.

"HACHI-KO"

There is a very famous story that endears many to the Akita. In the 1930s there was a dog named "Hachi-Ko," who each day would go to the local train station to meet his beloved owner, Professor Uneo, who arrived on the evening train from work. On one occasion his master did not arrive, having suffered a fatal heart attack while at work. Such was the dog's loyalty to his master that he sat and waited daily at the station for his master's return.

Although commuters had accepted the dog's daily presence as natural, everyone was terribly saddened by the sight of the faithful dog waiting for his master. No doubt, many wished for a way to tell the dog that his master would never again arrive on the train. Every day, the big Akita met the train and watched hopefully as the passengers stepped down from the train. Day by day, he grew thinner and ever more depressed.

Commuters brought him food and finally the station master provided him with a bed, but Hachi-Ko took no comfort in their attentions. His owner's former gardener took the dog in, but it was not Hachi-Ko's home. Gradually he began to spend more and more time at the station. Dr. Itagaki, a veterinarian and good friend of Professor Uneo, provided medical attention as required. Hachi-Ko grew older. He waited.

By 1932 the press had picked up his story and a bronze statue was commissioned in honor of his fidelity. The Society for the Preservation of Japanese Dogs unveiled the statue in April 1934. Shibuya Station commuters and onlookers were suitably impressed, but the old dog was

Author Meg Purnell-Carpenter poses with the bronze statue of Hachi-Ko. The Society for the Preservation of Japanese Dogs originally unveiled the statue to Hachi-Ko in April 1934 in the Shibuya Station Square.

not. The bronze monument did nothing to lift his unbearable sadness. Still he waited.

He died the following year at 11 years of age, which is not really old for an Akita, but Hachi-Ko had been too lonely for too many years. The statue of Hachi-Ko is still in the same place today, although the original was melted down to make ammunition during the war. After the war, the son of the original sculptor was commissioned to recreate the statue. School children sent monies and the statue was rebuilt in the same place at Shibuya Station Square. Hachi-Ko was "home again," and it brought a measure of reassurance that all would be right with the world. Today he looks with unblinking wonder at the modern world around him.

He was no show dog, but he sits in the square outside the station, with his one soft ear, seeming to observe all that comes and goes to the station. Many people touch his likeness for luck, and it is now well worn and smooth in places. As a further mark of respect, Hachi-Ko is now

Japan's fondness for its great Akitas is evident in modern-day Tokyo and other cities in Japan. Hachi-Ko's statue is flanked by a huge marble mosaic depicting Akitas of all ages.

flanked by a huge marble mosaic depicting Akitas of all ages.

This unique meeting place is called Hachi-Ko Plaza, and it has become a meeting place for businessmen and a place for lovers. It was, in fact, young students of Tokyo University who finally realized that something wasn't quite right. There was one more thing that must be done in order that Hachi-Ko might finally be at peace. In 1983 the students carried a bust of Professor Uneo from the school and placed it next to the statue of Hachi-Ko. Man and dog were finally reunited and in a respectful and simple ceremony conducted by the students;

a story of undying loyalty received a postscript. Hachi-Ko was finally at rest next to his beloved master.

IS THE AKITA FOR YOU?
Today we are asked, what is the breed like to live with? Both authors are great believers that a dog is what you make it. Having said that, this breed is different. It is strong in character, feels no pain or at least does not admit to it, can be stubborn (usually is!) but is highly intelligent and is extremely clean with very little doggy smell.

The Akita is a dog with a strong sense of self-importance; thus, it tends to dominate all other dogs. It is imperative that firm discipline is established from a very early age. This does not mean hitting or beating. The breed does tend to be dominant towards other dogs, so control is important. Training classes are vital for early socialization. If you can find outdoor training sessions, so much the better. You will find on average that the breed is highly intelligent, with males being more dominant than bitches but not necessarily quicker to learn.

For first-time Akita owners, we strongly recommend that you purchase a bitch, but don't think that will guarantee complete success. Unless you follow the guidelines in this book and those given by the breeder of your dog,

THE CAT'S MEOW
Although not related to the feline species, the Akita shares many attributes with the cat. He is extraordinarily clean in the house. He often cleans himself with his paws and buries his feces just like a cat. Similar to a cat's penchant for the aquatic, the Akita will instinctively choose fish over steak, though, true to his Nipponese beginnings, he also loves rice and fruit! Just as most cats hate water, the Akita does not like to swim even though he is strong and buoyant in the water. Akitas are dignified enough to endure comparison to the feline, but, for the record, most Akitas are not terribly fond of kitties.

it may not promise successful ownership. Remember that it is an understanding of the breed coupled with good common sense that are required of the Akita owner. It is advised that you talk to breeders and establish a rapport with the person from whom you buy your pup. The time you spend getting to know and understand your dog can make a large difference in your relationship with your Akita. Each dog is an individual and the Akita is often a little more individualistic than you might expect!

Akitas do not respond well to the constant repetition required for competitive obedience and can therefore be a bit of a puzzle for novice trainers. He is quite likely to want an explanation for everything. A repetitive formal training class can be quite boring for a highly intelligent dog who is a very quick learner. The "strange ways" of trainers, with all of their commands and methods, cannot make much sense to the Akita. He will wonder why you choose to go 'round and 'round in circles, stopping every minute and expecting him to sit. He must also wonder why his two-legged friend tires so easily and needs to stop and sit. If that be so, can you imagine his puzzlement when his human immediately insists on walking again before having rested?

In order to effectively train a dog that is dominant and used to

DOGS, DOGS, GOOD FOR YOUR HEART!

People usually purchase dogs for companionship, but studies show that dogs can help to improve their owners' health and level of activity, as well as lower a human's risk of coronary heart disease. Without even realizing it, when a person puts time into exercising, grooming and feeding a dog, he also puts more time into his own personal health care. Dog owners establish more routine schedules for their dogs to follow, which can have positive effects on their own health. Dogs also teach us patience, offer unconditional love and provide the joy of having a furry friend to pet!

working out things on his own, the trainer must be smarter than the dog! The best lesson here is not to bore the dog. Keep him guessing to maintain the delicate balance

TAKING CARE

Science is showing that as people take care of their pets, the pets are taking care of their owners. A recent study published in the *American Journal of Cardiology,* found that having a pet can prolong his owner's life. Pet owners generally have lower blood pressure, and pets help their owners to relax and keep more physically fit. It was also found that pets help to keep the elderly connected to their communities.

between requiring compliance and quick response to your commands and showing respect for his perceptiveness. Remember, the Akita is not a breed that will go overboard to please you as will, for instance, the Border Collie. He has been bred to think for himself and to be stubbornly persistent in his purpose.

Akitas are willing to indulge their owners, but only to a point. After about 10 or 15 minutes of repetitive training, especially in the heat of the day, the Akita is quite likely to sit down and say to his master, "You go ahead and when you've decided where we're going, come back and get me. In the meantime I'll just sit here and do my best to ignore your confusion."

The Akita is possessive of family and territory, and usually displays strong guarding instincts and the boldness to bite if his family is threatened. It should be noted, however, that almost any report of an Akita's biting is the result of irresponsible ownership and the failure of the owner to understand and properly control his Akita. The breed is not at fault here—it is lack of education and information that should always be forthcoming from any responsible breeder. As popularity grows, health and temperament must be of primary concern. The character of a proud and dominant breed can be eroded away by irresponsible breeding.

Each breed has a distinguishing personality as well as physical characteristics. Breeders should not attempt to change the Akita into a 100-pound lap dog or the breed will be forever lost to those who appreciate a dignified, discriminating, brave, stable and innately unique guard-companion.

As Mrs. Purnell-Carpenter stresses, one must screen all breeding stock for the appropriate problems. Unfortunately, not every breeder does this, but members of the breed clubs are required to abide by their Code of Ethics, which states that all stock must be tested for inherited conditions before breeding from them. It would be an excellent idea for the American Kennel Club to somehow have tighter control over animals that fail these examinations so that they cannot be bred from.

As Mrs. Purnell-Carpenter has frequently stated, "What is meant by good temperament? The Akita is not a lap dog, so please don't try and change him into one. One of the greatest attractions to the breed for me is its wonderful dignity. The only problem with temperament with our breed is unsuitable owners and indiscrimi-

The female Akita is a patient and protective baby-sitter.

nate breeders who do not bother to educate or inform potential puppy owners of the strength of character that this breed proudly possesses. When he sets his mind to something, the Akita is more likely to achieve it than is the average dog."

The Akita is highly intelligent and if he wants, for example, to escape from your yard, he will succeed. However, typical of the breed, he will probably only come to find you. Akitas are very clever at working out problems, puzzles and what's inside the refrigerator! Can dogs reason? Some authorities say no. Can Akitas reason? The authors say emphatically, yes!

Admittedly, there are some troublesome aspects associated with owning an Akita. One is his size. To someone cuddling a 15-

SKIN PROBLEMS

Eczema and dermatitis are skin problems that occur in many breeds, and they can often be tricky problems to solve. Frequently bathing the dog will remove skin oils and will cause the problem to worsen. Allergies to food or to something in the environment can also cause the problem. Consider trying homeopathic remedies in addition to seeing your veterinarian for direction.

pound puppy, understanding that the teddy bear in your arms will grow into a huge bear of over 100 pounds is often overlooked.

Will he be welcomed in every establishment? Not likely. His size alone is intimidating and that he resembles the "wolf" side of dogdom can be problematic for the public. If he had huge baby eyes, huge floppy ears and a cute little turned-up button nose, he would appeal to and not threaten most humans. He has small piercing eyes, pointy ears, a muzzle like that of a wolf and obviously big strong teeth—and his luxuriant "pelt" instinctively makes us aware of the wild side of the domesticated canine. It is these lupine attributes that evoke instinctive fear in humans, who grew up hearing rhyming couplets about the "big bad wolf."

Therefore, if you want a dog to hold in your arms or to be welcomed to lie quietly at your feet while you sip coffee at an outdoor cafe, choose another breed. On the other hand, if you want a dog that evokes awe and fascination in the very soul of your fellow man, by all means, choose the Akita!

And speaking of that lavish coat... should I tell you that the luxuriant soft puppy coat will eventually fall out? That's right— it will turn into hairballs that can always be found under the sofa, except when your mother-in-law

SILENCE OF THE BEARS

Like the other Japanese spitz breeds, Akitas are very quiet. When the Akita barks, there is reason to investigate.

is knocking at the door. Of course, then the hair floats out into the middle of the room or right onto the icing of the cake that you just prepared.

The good news regarding size is that Akitas require less food in proportion to their weight than do many other large breeds. Nonetheless, what goes in must come out. A large-size pooper-scooper is advised. The good side of the coin is that, like most other Oriental breeds, the Akita is exceptionally clean and rarely soils his surroundings. Most Oriental breeds, even the Toy breeds, are extraordinarily clean. They do very well in an apartment, not requiring a tremendous amount of exercise, but, like all other dogs, they must be taken out to relieve themselves at least four times per day. They can be paper-trained at a young age, but one should have a large reserve of newspapers and, as soon as possible, move the papers to the selected area outside. If given reasonable opportunity to eliminate outside, the Akita will select a spot as far away from the dwelling as possible, preferably a secluded corner of his fenced yard. Having christened that spot as the toilet area, he will return to it each time. Knowing where his toilet is located is necessary to make the chore of cleaning up much simpler for the owner.

Owners who live in the city soon learn which are the preferred toilet stops along the dog's daily walking route. Remember to always carry a pooper-scooper with which to clean up after your dog. Urination will be frequent and happen at the first opportunity, but owners should note that a certain amount of physical activity is required in order to effectively move the bowels, thus a brisk walk or jog will bring "results" quicker than will a leisurely stroll.

Owners tend to thwart the elimination process and then be angry at the dog if a mistake occurs in the house while the owner is away. Imagine, if you will, someone rushing you during your morning routine. It is distracting and quite likely to result in your forgetting something or being unable to complete the routine. So, if it is raining, take rain gear with you and be prepared to spend a few wet minutes walking the dog. If you are about to be late to work, call your employer and confess. Don't sentence the dog to a day of utter misery because you overslept!

Traits that should be distinct in the adult Akita are quiet dignity, an unruffled attitude,

When searching for your Akita puppy, you can judge breeders by the cleanliness and professionalism of their establishments. Do your homework before you go puppy shopping.

acceptance of your friends and suspicion of strangers. He is never a complainer and should demonstrate tolerance and silent acceptance of uncomfortable situations. The Akita should not be a barker and thus, in spite of his size, is an ideal choice for the apartment dweller.

When all of his many characteristics are put together in an ideal Akita package, he is an independent-thinking, imaginative creature who seeks action and challenge. If the Akita were human, he would be pushing a jet to its limits or diving the ocean floor or riding bulls in a rodeo! He is a leader—he is curious, self-willed and, let's face it, the kind of "person" about whom books are written and legends are born!

Our combined hopes for the breed's future must be that we will have less commercially minded people breeding litter after litter to supplement their retirement savings. We trust that more breeders will be truly dedicated to breeding selectively to maintain the true Akita type and character. Our fears would be that the breed becomes so over-popular and over-bred that we would lose the true character and breed type of the Akita. What a tremendous loss to all that would be!

AKITAS AND CHILDREN

If your Akita was raised with youngsters, the exuberant squealing and mock fights that occur between rambunctious children will be understood. If you have no children but understand the importance of a well-socialized, well-rounded adult dog, then take the time (while he's a puppy) to introduce him to well-behaved children. Walk him through a park where children play. Let him get used to hearing them squeal in fun. Take him to the football field

BODY GUARDS

Akitas are strongly protective of family and territory. Therefore, they are not inclined to stray away from their own territory.

so that he understands that the loud screams mean fun. Be sure to take along treats that he likes, tiny tidbits of food that you can secretly hand to the children so they can "feed the doggie," thereby establishing a friendly relationship with the children. Perhaps you have relatives who will visit with their hopefully well-mannered offspring. Above all, do not subject your young Akita to teasing or "smothering" by unruly children. It is sure to leave a lasting and unfavorable impression on the dog.

If your dog has not grown up with children, it is advisable to closely supervise his contact upon the arrival of friends with children. How can your dog understand that cousin Harry isn't really killing your six-year-old niece Victoria? When Harry chases her with his toy gun and she squeals "Help!", your Akita's protective instinct may take over, causing him to attempt to stop Harry from attacking the other child. In other words, dogs simply behave like dogs, and, in fact, the wild canine, the common example being the wolf, has a very highly developed social structure that is respectful of the elderly and protective of the young.

THE NEXT STEP
Should an Akita appeal to you as your next pet, then accept the sensible advice contained herein. Stick to the basic requirements—discipline, love, socialization and training. Allow for their slight stubbornness and remember that their eyes are the windows to their hearts and souls. If you can accept all of these things, welcome to Akita companionship. It is a wonderful breed to live with and it will remain loyal to you for life.

Even Akita pups are protective of their homes, always alert and ready to react to the slightest disturbance in their environments.

BREED STANDARD FOR THE

AKITA

MEETING THE IDEAL

The American Kennel Club defines a standard as: "A description of the ideal dog of each recognized breed, to serve as an ideal against which dogs are judged at shows." This "blueprint" is drawn up by the breed's recognized parent club, approved by a majority of its membership, and then submitted to the AKC for approval. This is a complete departure from the way standards are handled in England, where all standards and changes are controlled by The Kennel Club.

The AKC states that "An understanding of any breed must begin with its standard. This applies to all dogs, not just those intended for showing." The picture that the standard draws of the dog's type, gait, temperament and structure is the guiding image used by breeders as they plan their programs.

Each breed approved by the American Kennel Club has a standard that provides a word picture of what the specific breed should look like. All reputable breeders strive to produce animals that will meet the requirements of the standard. Many breeds were developed for a specific purpose, e.g., herding, retrieving, going to ground, guarding or pure companionship. The Akita originally was bred to be a hunter.

In addition to describing the breed's appearance, the standard indicates the desirable Akita personality, disposition and intelligence sought after in the breed.

Standards were originally written by dog people who had a love and a concern for the breed as well as a basic knowledge of the function of an animal's anatomy. In designing the standard, they strove to preserve the essential characteristics of the Akita that were unlike those of any other breed, insisting that care be taken to maintain these characteristics through the generations.

As time progressed, dog breeders became aware that

certain areas of the dog needed more specific description or definition. Many standards were "fleshed out" with more detail and elaboration. However, standards for any breed are never changed on a whim, and serious study and exchange between breeders take place before any move is made. Following is the standard drawn up by the Akita Club of America and approved by the AKC.

THE AMERICAN KENNEL CLUB STANDARD FOR THE AKITA

General Appearance: Large, powerful, alert, with much substance and heavy bone. The broad head, forming a blunt triangle, with deep muzzle, small eyes and erect ears carried forward in line with back of neck, is characteristic of the breed. The large, curled tail, balancing the broad head, is also characteristic of the breed.

Head: Massive but in balance with body; free of wrinkle when at ease. Skull flat between ears and broad; jaws square and powerful with minimal dewlap. Head forms a blunt triangle when viewed from above. *Fault*— Narrow or snipy head. *Muzzle*— Broad and full. Distance from nose to stop is to distance from stop to occiput as 2 is to 3. *Stop*—

BREEDER'S BLUEPRINT
If you are considering breeding your bitch, it is very important that you are familiar with the breed standard. Reputable breeders breed with the intention of producing dogs that are as close as possible to the standard and that contribute to the advancement of the breed. Study the standard for both physical appearance and temperament, and make certain your bitch and your chosen stud dog measure up.

Well defined, but not too abrupt. A shallow furrow extends well up forehead. *Nose*—Broad and black. Liver permitted on white Akitas, but black always preferred. *Disqualification*—Butterfly nose or total lack of pigmentation on nose. *Ears*—The ears of the Akita are characteristic of the breed. They are strongly erect and small in relation to rest of head. If ear is folded forward for measuring length, tip will touch upper eye rim. Ears are triangular, slightly rounded at tip, wide at base, set wide on head but not too low, and carried slightly forward over eyes in line with back of neck. *Disqualification*—Drop or broken

The breed standard informs the judge's opinion during a conformation show. How closely the Akita "conforms" to the standard determines how well the dog does in competition.

ears. *Eyes*—Dark brown, small, deep-set and triangular in shape. Eye rims black and tight. *Lips and Tongue*—Lips black and not pendulous; tongue pink. *Teeth*—Strong with scissors bite preferred, but level bite acceptable. *Disqualification*—Noticeably undershot or overshot.

Neck and Body: *Neck*—Thick and muscular; comparatively short, widening gradually toward shoulders. A pronounced crest blends in with base of skull. *Body*—Longer than high, as 10 is to 9 in males; 11 to 9 in bitches. Chest wide and deep; depth of chest is one-half height of dog at shoulder. Ribs well sprung, brisket well developed. Level back with firmly-muscled loin and moderate tuck-up. Skin pliant but not loose. *Serious Faults*—Light bone, rangy body.

Tail: Large and full, set high and carried over back or against flank in a three-quarter, full, or double curl, always dipping to or below level of back. On a three-quarter curl, tip drops well down flank. Root large and strong. Tail bone reaches hock when let down. Hair coarse, straight and full, with no appearance of a plume. *Disqualification*—Sickle or uncurled tail.

Forequarters and Hindquarters: *Forequarters*—Shoulders strong and powerful with moderate layback. Forelegs heavy-boned and straight as viewed from front. Angle of pastern 15 degrees forward from vertical. *Faults*—Elbows in or out, loose shoulders. *Hindquarters*—Width, muscular development and bone comparable to forequarters. Upper thighs well developed. Stifle moderately

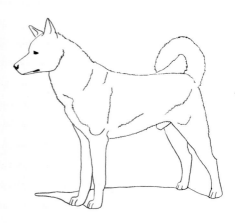

Correct profile of the Akita.

Incorrect profile: poor angulation; straight front and rear quarters; overall lack of substance; poor tailset and carriage.

Head of good proportions; proper ear size and carriage.

Incorrect head: muzzle too long; ears large and set too far apart; backskull too long and flat.

Headstudy of the Akita.

Author Meg Purnell-Carpenter, judging a national specialty show in Japan.

bent and hocks well let down, turning neither in nor out. *Dewclaws*—On front legs generally not removed; dewclaws on hind legs generally removed. *Feet*—Cat feet, well knuckled up with thick pads. Feet straight ahead.

The Akita's gait reveals the dog's sound structure and, for many judges, is the most important feature of the breed. Too often, however, judges forget that Akitas are not supposed to move like the Poodle or Springer Spaniel. This is a heavy dog whose back must remain level when single-tracking.

Coat: Double-coated. Undercoat thick, soft, dense and shorter than outer coat. Outer coat straight, harsh and standing somewhat off body. Hair on head, legs and ears short. Length of hair at withers and rump approximately two inches, which is slightly longer than on rest of body, except tail, where coat is longest and most profuse. *Fault*—Any indication of ruff or feathering.

Color: Any color including white; brindle; or pinto. Colors are brilliant and clear and markings are well balanced, with or without mask or blaze. White Akitas have no mask. Pinto has a white background with large, evenly placed patches covering head and more than one-third of body. Undercoat may be a different color from outer coat.

Gait: Brisk and powerful with strides of moderate length. Back remains strong, firm and level. Rear legs move in line with front legs.

Size: Males 26 to 28 inches at the withers; bitches 24 to 26 inches. *Disqualification*—dogs under 25 inches; bitches under 23 inches.

Temperament: Alert and responsive, dignified and courageous. Aggressive toward other dogs.

Approved December 12, 1972

AKITA

WHERE TO BEGIN?

If you are convinced that the Akita is the ideal dog for you, it's time to learn about where to find a puppy and what to look for. Locating a litter of Akitas should not present a problem for the new owner. You should inquire about breeders in your area who enjoy a good reputation in the breed. Knowing the type Akita that you like, whether it's the larger American-type dog, the very typey Japanese dog or a "blend" of the two, will help you in locating a line of Akitas that you find appealing. Regardless of which type you prefer, you are looking for an established breeder with outstanding dog ethics and a strong commitment to the Akita breed. New owners should have as many questions as they have doubts. An established breeder is indeed the one to answer your four million questions and make you comfortable with your choice of the Akita. An established breeder will sell you a puppy at a fair price if, and only if, the breeder determines that you are a suitable, worthy owner of his dogs. An established

TEMPERAMENT COUNTS

Your selection of a good puppy can be determined by your needs. A show potential or a good pet? It is your choice. Every puppy, however, should be of good temperament. Although show-quality puppies are bred and raised with emphasis on physical conformation, responsible breeders strive for equally good temperament. Do not buy from a breeder who concentrates solely on physical beauty at the expense of personality.

ARE YOU PREPARED?

Unfortunately, when a puppy is bought by someone who does not take into consideration the time and attention that dog ownership requires, it is the puppy who suffers when he is either abandoned or placed in a shelter by a frustrated owner. So all of the "homework" you do in preparation for your pup's arrival will benefit you both. The more informed you are, the more you will know what to expect and the better equipped you will be to handle the ups and downs of raising a puppy. Hopefully, everyone in the household is willing to do his part in raising and caring for the pup. The anticipation of owning a dog often brings a lot of promises from excited family members: "I will walk him every day," "I will feed him," "I will house-train him," etc., but these things take time and effort, and promises can easily be forgotten once the novelty of the new pet has worn off.

breeder can be relied upon for advice, no matter what time of day or night. A reputable breeder will accept a puppy back, without questions, should you decide that this is not the right dog for you.

Choosing a breeder is an important first step in dog ownership. Fortunately, the majority of Akita breeders is devoted to the breed and its well-being. Discuss the various health concerns that are hereditary in the Akita. Surely your chosen breeder will be screening for various health problems, including hip dysplasia, hypothyroidism, von Willebrand's disease and progressive retinal atrophy. New owners should know about these conditions and how they affect the Akita.

You should have little problem finding a reputable breeder who doesn't live in another state or on the other side of the country. The American Kennel Club is able to recommend breeders of quality Akitas, as can any local all-breed club or Akita club. Potential owners are encouraged to attend dog shows to see the Akitas in action, to meet the owners and handlers firsthand and to get an idea of what Akitas look like outside a photographer's lens. Provided you approach the handlers when they are not terribly busy with the dogs, most are more than willing to answer questions, recommend breeders and give advice.

Once you have contacted and met a breeder or two and made your choice about which breeder is best suited to your needs, it's time to visit the litter. Keep in mind that many top breeders have waiting lists. Sometimes new owners have to wait as long as two years for a puppy. If you are really committed to the breeder whom you've selected, then you will wait (and hope for an early arrival!). If not, you may have to resort to your second-choice breeder or another breeder working from the same lines.

Since you are likely to be choosing an Akita as a pet dog and not a show dog, you simply should select a pup that is friendly and attractive. The average litter size for Akitas is 7 or 8 pups, however, litters of 15 have been documented, so the selection of puppies, colors and

personalities should be considerable with most litters. The older the breeding partners, the smaller will be the litter, generally speaking. For breeders, it is considered wise to breed a virgin bitch to an experienced stud dog and vice-versa.

Color is not an important consideration with the Akita. Given the many attractive color possibilities and patterns, each Akita is unique unto itself. If you are buying a show dog that you wish to exhibit internationally, color does play a more significant role. FCI shows do not

Although white is not a popular color for the Akita, it is a perfectly acceptable and handsome choice.

KENNEL BLINDNESS

Not a disease that affects the dog's body, kennel blindness is a contagious disorder that affects dog breeders. Simply defined, the breeder cannot see any flaws in his own dogs but can spot one in another kennel's dog from 100 yards! Be forewarned—not every breeder can see clearly, so bring your commonsense spectacles!

DID YOU KNOW?

Akitas are free whelpers who are quite capable of delivering without human intervention. First-time mothers can be a bit clumsy with a large litter, so that is the time when breeders necessarily offer human assistance. When she is getting back into her nest, turning around and around, it is wise to be there to make sure she does not step on a whelp or lie down on one. She is so large, and newborns are rather small, so it could happen that she would lie back on one and not know what she is unintentionally smothering the poor thing.

permit black-masked dogs to compete as Japanese Akitas, though most black-masked dogs are of American type, which at FCI shows are classified as Great Japanese Dogs—a terribly generic name to call such truly great

dogs. Likewise, the type of Akita that you buy will affect which class you can enter with your "Akita."

In terms of the sex of your puppy, there are some differences to consider beyond the mere size of the two. Males are, of course, larger than females, stronger in muscle mass and somewhat more dominant, which is not to say that the female Akita cannot and will not stridently defend her property and her superiority. Make no mistake that she will!

Although there are exceptions to every commonly held concept, the female will be more patient and gentle with small children. She is genetically programmed to be that way, as are the females of most species. The male's job is to acquire a mate, to fight to defend her and his territory (or his pack, which would be you and your family) and, generally, to keep his pack in order. Without proper upbringing to make the Akita understand that he is a pack member and not the leader of your family pack, he can sometimes attempt to take on more responsibility than you would prefer.

The Akita is slow to mature and is not to be considered adult until well over two years of age. Physically, the males will continue to build muscle and mass until over five years, whereas females will usually finish out their physical development within six months of having whelped their first litter.

Breeders commonly allow visitors to see the litter by around the fifth or sixth week, and puppies leave for their new homes around the eighth week. Breeders who permit their puppies to leave early are more interested in your money than their puppies' well-being. Puppies need to learn the rules of the pack from their dams, and most dams continue teaching the pups manners and dos and don'ts until around the eighth week.

Breeders spend significant amounts of time with the Akita toddlers so that they are able to interact with the "other species," i.e., humans. Given the long history that dogs and humans have, bonding between the two species is natural but must be nurtured. A well-bred, well-socialized Akita pup wants nothing more than to be near you.

COMMITMENT OF OWNERSHIP

After considering all of these factors, you have most likely already made some very important decisions about selecting your puppy. You have chosen an Akita, which means that you have decided which characteristics you want in a dog and what type of dog will best fit into your family and lifestyle. If you have selected a breeder, you have gone a step

further—you have done your research and found a responsible, conscientious person who breeds sound, healthy Akitas and who should be a reliable source of help as you and your puppy adjust to life together. If you have observed a litter in action, you have obtained a firsthand look at the dynamics of a puppy "pack" and, thus, you should learn about each pup's individual personality—

PUPPY APPEARANCE

Your puppy should have a well-fed appearance but not a distended abdomen, which may indicate worms or incorrect feeding, or both. The body should be firm, with a solid feel. The skin of the abdomen should be pale pink and clean, without signs of scratching or rash. Check the hind legs to make certain that dewclaws were removed. Front dewclaws are usually not removed on Akita pups.

BOY OR GIRL?

An important consideration to be discussed is the sex of your puppy. For a family companion, a bitch may be the better choice, considering the female's inbred concern for all young creatures and her accompanying tolerance and patience. It is always advisable to spay a pet bitch or neuter a pet male, which may guarantee her a longer life.

playful, friendly, aggressive, etc. Equally as important, you will learn to recognize what a healthy pup should look and act like. All of these things will help you in your search, and when you find the Akita that was meant for you, you will know it!

Researching your breed, selecting a responsible breeder and observing as many pups as possible are all important steps on the way to dog ownership. It may seem like a lot of effort...and you have not even taken the pup home yet! Remember, though, you cannot be too careful when it comes to deciding on the type of dog you want and finding out about your prospective pup's background. Buying a puppy is not—or should not be—just another whimsical purchase. This is one instance in which you actually do get to choose your own family! You may be thinking that buying a puppy should be fun—it should not be so serious and so much work. Keep in mind that your puppy is not a cuddly stuffed toy or decorative lawn ornament, but a creature that will become a real member of your family. You will come to realize that, while buying a puppy is a pleasurable and exciting endeavor, it is not something to be taken lightly. Relax...the fun will start when the pup comes home!

Always keep in mind that a puppy is nothing more than a

perhaps you have even found one that particularly appeals to you.

However, even if you have not yet found the Akita puppy of your dreams, observing pups will help you learn to recognize certain behavior and to determine what a pup's behavior indicates about his temperament. You will be able to pick out which pups are the leaders, which ones are less outgoing, which ones are confident, which ones are shy,

to be a well-adjusted and well-mannered adult dog—a dog that could be your most loyal friend.

Akitas grow up to be fabulous babysitters, as this proud nanny clearly displays.

PREPARING PUPPY'S PLACE IN YOUR HOME

Researching your breed and finding a breeder are only two aspects of the "homework" you will have to do before taking your Akita puppy home. You will also have to prepare your home and family for the new addition. Much as you baby in a furry disguise…a baby who is virtually helpless in a human world and who trusts his owner for fulfillment of his basic needs for survival. In addition to food, water and shelter, your pup needs care, protection, guidance and love. If you are not prepared to commit to this, then you are not ready to own a dog.

"Wait a minute," you say. "How hard could this be? All of my neighbors own dogs and they seem to be doing just fine. Why should I have to worry about all of this?" Well, you should not worry about it; in fact, you will probably find that once your Akita pup gets used to his new home, he will fall into his place in the family quite naturally. But it never hurts to emphasize the commitment of dog ownership. With some time and patience, it is really not too difficult to raise a curious and exuberant Akita pup

TIME TO GO HOME

Breeders rarely release puppies until they are eight weeks of age. This is an acceptable age for most breeds of dog, excepting Toy breeds, which are not released until around 12 weeks, given their petite sizes. If a breeder has a puppy that is 12 weeks of age or older, he is likely well socialized and house-trained. Be sure that he is otherwise healthy before deciding to take him home.

Finding his place in his new home, this young Akita is the picture of good health and alertness.

For the pet owner, a long-coated Akita puppy may be an excellent choice. Although long-coats cannot be exhibited, they make marvelous, attractive pets.

PET INSURANCE

Just like you can insure your car, your house and your own health, you likewise can insure your dog's health. Investigate a pet insurance policy by talking to your vet. Depending on the age of your dog, the breed and the kind of coverage you desire, your policy can be very affordable. Most policies cover accidental injuries, poisoning and thousands of medical problems and illnesses, including cancers. Some carriers also offer routine care and immunization coverage.

PEDIGREE VS. REGISTRATION CERTIFICATE

Too often new owners are confused between these two important documents. Your puppy's pedigree, essentially a family tree, is a written record of a dog's genealogy of three generations or more. The pedigree will show you the names as well as performance titles of all dogs in your pup's background. Your breeder must provide you with a registration application, with his part properly filled out. You must complete the application and send it to the AKC with the proper fee. Every puppy must come from a litter that has been AKC-registered by the breeder, born in the US and from a sire and dam that are also registered with the AKC.

The seller must provide you with complete records to identify the puppy. The AKC requires that the seller provide the buyer with the following: breed; sex, color and markings; date of birth; litter number (when available); names and registration numbers of the parents; breeder's name; and date sold or delivered.

he has a place that he can "call his own."

When you bring your new puppy into your home, you are bringing him into what will become his home as well. Obviously, you did not buy a puppy so that he could take over your house, but in order for a puppy to grow into a stable, well-adjusted dog, he has to feel comfortable in his surroundings. Remember, he is leaving the warmth and security of his mother and littermates, as well as the familiarity of the only place he has ever known, so it is important to make his transition

This young pup's ears are almost completely erect. Ask the breeder about his line and when to expect the ears to rise. Every line (and sometimes dog) is different.

would prepare a nursery for a newborn baby, you will need to designate a place in your home that will be the puppy's own. How you prepare your home will depend on how much freedom the dog will be allowed. Whatever you decide, you must ensure that

Your local pet shop will have a variety of crates from which you can choose the one which best suits your needs. A fiberglass crate is necessary for traveling by air.

PHOTO COURTESY OF DOSKOCIL

WHAT YOU SHOULD BUY

CRATE

To someone unfamiliar with the use of crates in dog training, it may seem like punishment to shut a dog in a crate, but this is not the case at all. Most breeders and trainers recommend crates as preferred tools for show puppies as well as pet puppies. Crates are not cruel—crates have many humane and highly effective uses in dog care and training. For example, crate training is a very popular and very successful house-training method. A crate can keep your dog safe during travel and, perhaps most importantly, a crate provides your dog with a place of his own in your home. It serves as a "doggie bedroom" of sorts—your Akita can curl up in his crate when he wants to sleep or when he just needs a break. Many dogs sleep in their crates overnight. With soft bedding and his favorite toy, a crate becomes a cozy pseudo-den for your dog. Like his ancestors, he too will seek out the comfort and retreat of a den—you just happen to be providing him with something a little more luxurious than what his early ancestors enjoyed.

An Akita should have a crate that is at least 30 inches long for the female, and 40 inches might be preferred for the male. It should be 22 to 24 inches in

as easy as possible. By preparing a place in your home for the puppy, you are making him feel as welcome as possible in a strange new place. It should not take him long to get used to it, but the sudden shock of being transplanted is somewhat traumatic for a young pup. Imagine how a small child would feel in the same situation—that is how your puppy must be feeling. It is up to you to reassure him and to let him know, "Little *inu*, you are going to like it here!"

width and 26 inches or more in height. Equally as important, the crate should be open so that the dog can see its surroundings, not closed in. Therefore, you need to purchase a wire crate for your Akita; a fiberglass crate is required by airlines for travel. Male Akitas in particular want to be able to control their surroundings, and being shut off is apt to make him act aggressively with barking and foolishness in an attempt to convince the world that although he can't see it, he is indeed in control!

BEDDING
A soft crate pad in the dog's crate will help the dog feel more at home and you may also like to provide a small blanket. This will take the place of the leaves, twigs, etc., that the pup would use in the wild to make a den; the pup can make his own "burrow" in the crate. Although your pup is somewhat removed from his den-making ancestors, the denning instinct is still a part of his genetic makeup. Second, until you take your pup home, he has been sleeping amid the warmth of his mother and litter-mates, and while a blanket is not the same as a warm, breathing body, it still provides heat and something with which to snuggle. You will want to wash your pup's bedding frequently in case he has an accident in his crate,

CRATE-TRAINING TIPS
During crate training, you should partition off the section of the crate in which the pup stays. If he is given too big an area, this will hinder your training efforts. Crate training is based on the fact that a dog does not like to soil his sleeping quarters, so it is ineffective to keep a pup in an area that is so big that he can eliminate in one end and get far enough away from it to sleep. Also, you want to make the crate den-like for the pup. Blankets and a favorite toy will make the crate cozy for the small pup; as he grows, you may want to evict some of his "roommates" to make more room. It will take some coaxing at first, but be patient. Given some time to get used to it, your pup will adapt to his new home-within-a-home quite nicely.

FEEDING TIPS

You will probably start feeding your pup the same food that he has been getting from the breeder; the breeder should give you a few days' supply to start you off. Although you should not give your pup too many treats, you will want to have puppy treats on hand for coaxing, training, rewards, etc. Be careful, though, as a small pup's calorie requirements are relatively low and a few treats can add up to almost a full day's worth of calories without the required nutrition.

Puppies like soft toys for chewing. Because they are teething, soft items like stuffed toys soothe their aching gums. Be especially careful when your Akita pup has a soft toy!

and replace or remove any blanket that becomes ragged and starts to fall apart.

Toys

Toys are a must for dogs of all ages, especially for curious playful pups. Puppies are the "children" of the dog world, and what child does not love toys? Chew toys provide enjoyment for both dog and owner—your dog will enjoy playing with his favorite toys, while you will enjoy the fact that they distract him from your expensive shoes and leather sofa. Puppies love to chew; in fact, chewing is a physical need for pups as they are teething, and everything looks appetizing! The full range of your possessions— from old glove to Oriental carpet—are fair game in the eyes of a teething pup. Puppies are not all that discerning when it comes to finding something to literally "sink their teeth into"—everything tastes great!

All Akitas need something upon which to have chewing exercise and stress relief. Those dogs who spend a great deal of time alone must have a variety of

new toys and bones to avoid and relieve boredom. Remember that soft rubber toys, especially those with squeakers inside, are not for the Akita and are to be avoided at all costs. If a pup "disembowels" a squeaky toy (and that's easy to do), the small plastic squeaker inside can be dangerous if swallowed. Likewise, stuffed toys will become de-stuffed in no time. The overly excited pup may ingest the stuffing, which is neither digestible nor nutritious.

The best "toy" is a fresh leg or knucklebone from the butcher but, failing that, give him a hard rubber or nylon toy. Monitor the condition of all your pup's toys carefully and get rid of any that have been chewed to the point of becoming potentially dangerous.

The authors recommend natural bones for Akitas, provided that you purchase the very largest bones that your butcher has and that you monitor the dog whenever he's chewing on the bone. Since natural bones can splinter, supervision is necessary. Natural bones are excellent forms of calcium and perfect for giving the Akita's teeth and jaws the exercise they need to develop properly and remain strong.

LEAD

A nylon lead is probably the best option as it is the most resistant to puppy teeth should your pup take a liking to chewing on his

TOYS, TOYS, TOYS!

With a big variety of dog toys available, and so many that look like they would be a lot of fun for a dog, be careful in your selection. It is amazing what a set of puppy teeth can do to an innocent-looking toy, so, obviously, safety is a major consideration. Be sure to choose the most durable products that you can find. Hard nylon bones and toys are a safe bet, and many of them are offered in different scents and flavors that will be sure to capture your dog's attention. It is always fun to play a game of fetch with your dog, and there are balls and flying discs that are specially made to withstand dog teeth.

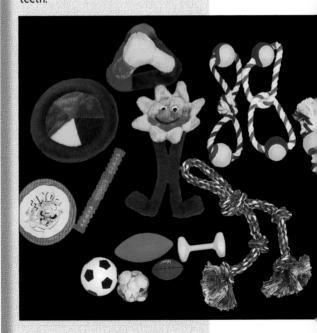

through the strong nylon. Nylon leads are also lightweight, which is good for a young Akita who is just getting used to the idea of walking on a lead. For the adult dog, a sturdy leather lead is necessary since the Akita is a strong dog who will run away when the opportunity presents itself.

COLLAR

Your pup should get used to wearing a collar all the time since you will want to attach his ID tags to it. Plus, you have to attach the lead to something! A lightweight nylon collar is a good

As your Akita grows up, you will have to acquire a stronger lead for everyday walks.

PLAY'S THE THING

Teaching the puppy to play with his toys in running and fetching games is an ideal way to help the puppy develop muscle, learn motor skills and bond with you, his owner and master. He also needs to learn how to inhibit his bite reflex and never to use his teeth on people, forbidden objects and other animals in play. Whenever you play with your puppy, you make the rules. This becomes an important message to your puppy in teaching him that you are the pack leader and control everything he does in life. Once your dog accepts you as his leader, your relationship with him will be cemented for life.

lead. Of course, this is a habit that should be nipped in the bud, but if your pup likes to chew on his lead he has a very slim chance of being able to chew

be fed and where he will be spending time. Stainless steel or sturdy plastic bowls are popular choices. Plastic bowls are more chewable. Dogs tend not to chew on the steel variety, which can be sterilized. It is important to buy sturdy bowls since anything is in danger of being chewed by puppy teeth and you do not want your dog to be constantly chewing apart his bowl (for his safety and for your purse!).

Your local pet shop will have a large selection of leads from which you may choose the ones that best suit your needs.

choice; make sure that it fits snugly enough so that the pup cannot wriggle out of it, but is loose enough so that it will not be uncomfortably tight around the pup's neck. You should be able to fit a finger between the pup and the collar. It may take some time for your pup to get used to wearing the collar, but soon he will not even notice that it is there. Choke collars are made for training, but should only be used by an experienced handler. Never use a chain collar on an Akita, since it will damage the coat around the neck and cause skin irritation.

FOOD AND WATER BOWLS
Your pup will need two bowls, one for food and one for water. You may want two sets of bowls, one for inside and one for outside, depending on where the dog will

MENTAL AND DENTAL
Toys not only help your puppy get the physical and mental stimulation he needs but also provide a great way to keep his teeth clean. Hard rubber or nylon toys, especially those constructed with grooves, are designed to scrape away plaque, preventing bad breath and gum infection.

CHOOSE AN APPROPRIATE COLLAR

The BUCKLE COLLAR is the standard collar used for everyday purpose. Be sure that you adjust the buckle on growing puppies. Check it every day. It can become too tight overnight! These collars can be made of leather or nylon. Attach your dog's identification tags to this collar.

The CHOKE COLLAR is the usual collar recommended for training. It is constructed of highly polished steel so that it slides easily through the stainless steel loop. The idea is that the dog controls the pressure around its neck and he will stop pulling if the collar becomes uncomfortable. Never use a chain choke on your Akita.

The HALTER is for a trained dog that has to be restrained to prevent running away, chasing a cat and the like. Considered the most humane of all collars, it is frequently used on smaller dogs for which collars are not comfortable.

Akita owners should invest in bowl stands for their dogs. These stands elevate the dog's food and water bowls so that the Akita does not have to crane his neck to reach them. Some studies have shown that bowl stands are effective in warding off bloat, a potentially deadly condition caused by the dog's gulping air while eating. The term "bloat" refers to the condition of the dog's stomach, which expands like a balloon because the stomach twists and air cannot escape.

CLEANING SUPPLIES

Until a pup is house-trained, you will be doing a lot of cleaning. "Accidents" will occur, which is acceptable in the beginning because the puppy does not know any better. All you can do is be prepared to clean up any accidents. Old rags, towels, newspapers and a safe disinfectant are good to have on hand.

BEYOND THE BASICS

The items previously discussed are the bare necessities. You will find out what else you need as you go along—grooming supplies, flea/tick protection, baby gates to partition a room, etc. These things will vary depending on your situation but

Invest in a bowl stand for your Akita adolescent. The stand avoids the dog's having to crane his neck, therefore assisting with digestion and warding off bloat.

Your local pet shop sells an array of dishes and bowls for water and food. Purchase the largest, strongest bowls you can find.

it is important that you have everything you need to feed and make your Akita comfortable in his first few days at home.

PUPPY-PROOFING YOUR HOME

Aside from making sure that your Akita will be comfortable in your home, you also have to make sure that your home is safe for your Akita. This means taking precautions that your pup will not get into anything he should not get into and that there is nothing within his reach that may harm him should he

SKULL & CROSSBONES

Thoroughly puppy-proof your house before bringing your puppy home. Never use cockroach or rodent poisons or plant fertilizers in any area accessible to the puppy. Avoid the use of toilet cleaners. Most dogs are born with "toilet-bowl sonar" and will take a drink if the lid is left open. Also keep the trash secured and out of reach.

sniff it, chew it, inspect it, etc. This probably seems obvious since, while you are primarily concerned with your pup's safety, at the same time you do not want your belongings to be ruined. Breakables should be placed out of reach if your dog is to have full run of the house. If he is to be limited to certain places within the house, keep any potentially dangerous items in the "off-limits" areas. An electrical cord can pose a danger should the puppy decide to taste it—and who is going to convince a pup that it would not make a great chew toy? Cords should be fastened tightly against the wall. If your dog is going to spend time in a crate, make sure that

TOXIC PLANTS

Many plants can be toxic to dogs. If you see your dog carrying a piece of vegetation in his mouth, approach him in a quiet, disinterested manner, avoid eye contact, pet him and gradually remove the plant from his mouth. Alternatively, offer him a treat and maybe he'll drop the plant on his own accord. Be sure no toxic plants are growing in your own garden.

Purchase a king-size pooper-scooper for your noble bear dog!

there is nothing near his crate that he can reach if he sticks his curious little nose or paws through the openings. Just as you would with a child, keep all household cleaners and chemicals where the pup cannot reach them.

It is also important to make sure that the outside of your home is safe. Of course your puppy should never be unsuper-

NATURAL TOXINS

Examine your grass and landscaping before bringing your puppy home. Many varieties of plants have leaves, stems or flowers that are toxic if ingested, and you can depend on a curious puppy to investigate them. Ask your vet for information on poisonous plants or research them at your library.

vised, but a pup let loose in the yard will want to run and explore, and he should be granted that freedom. Do not let a fence give you a false sense of security; you would be surprised how crafty (and persistent) a dog can be in working out how to dig under and squeeze his way through small holes, or to jump

or climb over a fence. Be sure to repair or secure any gaps in the fence. Check the fence periodically to ensure that it is in good shape and make repairs as needed; a very determined pup may return to the same spot to "work on it" until he is able to get through.

Akitas are not high jumpers because of their great weight, but they can climb like chimpanzees! The young pup must never—repeat, *never!*—discover that he can escape from the yard. He must always be behind a fence that is beyond his ability to climb over. If this is so, he is unlikely to try to scale a 3-foot-high fence when he is grown because he was never able to do so as a puppy. But to be safe, it is best to fence your yard with fencing of a sufficient height to keep the dog securely inside.

The males disdain any sort of confinement that interferes with protecting their territory, and neither male nor female will want to be shut away outside when the family is inside. The job of male or female is to protect and comfort the family, and how can they do that if they are isolated outside?

FIRST TRIP TO THE VET

You have selected your puppy, and your home and family are ready. Now all you have to do is collect your Akita from the breeder and the fun begins, right? Well...not so fast. Something else you need to prepare is your pup's first trip to the veterinarian. Perhaps the breeder can recommend someone in the area who specializes in Akitas or other Northern or giant breeds, or maybe you know some other Akita owners who can suggest a good vet. Either way, you should have an appointment arranged for your pup before you pick him up.

The pup's first visit will consist of an overall examination to make sure that the pup does not have any problems that are not apparent to you. The veterinarian will also set up a schedule for the pup's vaccinations; the breeder will inform you of which

The Akita pup's curiosity rivals that of the cat! Keep breakables and valuables away from your adventurous Akita's nose and paws.

ones the pup has already received and the vet can continue from there.

INTRODUCTION TO THE FAMILY

Everyone in the house will be excited about the puppy's coming home and will want to pet him and play with him, but it is best to make the introduction low-key so as not to overwhelm the puppy. He is apprehensive already. It is the first time he has been separated from his dam and the breeder, and the ride to your home is likely to be the first time he has been in a car. The last thing you want to do is smother him, as this will only frighten him further. This is not to say that human contact is not extremely necessary at this stage, because this is the time when a connection between the pup and his human family is formed.

HOW VACCINES WORK

If you've just bought a puppy, you surely know the importance of having your pup vaccinated, but do you understand how vaccines work? Vaccines contain the same bacteria or viruses that cause the disease you want to prevent, but they have been chemically modified so that they don't cause any harm. Instead, the vaccine causes your dog to produce antibodies that fight the harmful bacteria. Thus, if your dog is exposed to the disease in the future, the antibodies will destroy the viruses or bacteria.

new noises, new smells and new things to investigate: so be gentle, be affectionate and be as comforting as you can be.

PUP'S FIRST NIGHT HOME

Puppies whine to let others know where they are and hopefully to get company out of it. Place your pup in his new bed or crate in his room and close the door.

Akitas do things at their own pace. Don't rush your puppy into too many new experiences on the first day in your home. He'll appreciate your patience.

Gentle petting and soothing words should help console him, as well as just putting him down and letting him explore on his own (under your watchful eye, of course).

The pup may approach the family members or may busy himself with exploring for a while. Gradually, each person should spend some time with the pup, one at a time, crouching down to get as close to the pup's level as possible and letting him sniff their hands and petting him gently. He definitely needs human attention and he needs to be touched—this is how to form an immediate bond. Just remember that the pup is experiencing a lot of things for the first time, at the same time. There are new people,

MANNERS MATTER

During the socialization process, a puppy should meet people, experience different environments and definitely be exposed to other canines. Through playing and interacting with other dogs, your puppy will learn lessons, ranging from controlling the pressure of his jaws by biting his littermates to the innerworkings of the canine pack that he will apply to his human relationships for the rest of his life. That is why removing a puppy from its litter too early (before eight weeks) can be detrimental to the pup's development.

THE RIDE HOME

Taking your dog from the breeder to your home in a car can be a very uncomfortable experience for both of you. The puppy will have been taken from his warm, friendly, safe environment and brought into a strange new environment—an environment that moves! Be prepared for loose bowels, urination, crying, whining and even fear biting. With proper love and encouragement when you arrive home, the stress of the trip should quickly disappear.

Mercifully, he may fall asleep without a peep. When the inevitable occurs, ignore the whining: he is fine. Be strong and keep his interest in mind. Do not allow yourself to feel guilty and visit the pup. He will fall asleep eventually.

Many breeders recommend placing a piece of bedding from his former home in his new bed so that he recognizes the scent of his littermates. Others still advise placing a hot water bottle in his bed for warmth. This latter may be a good idea provided the pup doesn't attempt to suckle—he'll get good and wet and may not fall asleep so fast.

Puppy's first night can be somewhat stressful for the pup and his new family. Remember that you are setting the tone of nighttime at your house. Unless you want to play with your pup at 10 p.m., midnight and 2 a.m., don't initiate the habit. Your family will thank you, and, in time, so will your pup!

PREVENTING PUPPY PROBLEMS

SOCIALIZATION

Now that you have done all of the preparatory work and have helped your pup get accustomed to his new home and family, it is about time for you to have some fun!

Given the opportunity, your Akita puppy will take over your home. He may even share his throne with you.

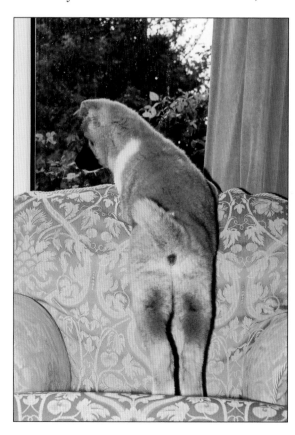

Akita puppies grow up to become very large, strong dogs. Just look at the size of the paws on this trio.

Socializing your Akita pup gives you the opportunity to show off your new friend, and your pup gets to reap the benefits of being an adorable furry creature that people will want to pet and, in general, think is absolutely precious!

Besides getting to know his new family, your puppy should be exposed to other people, animals and situations, but of course he must not come into close contact with dogs you don't know well until his course of injections is fully complete. Keep in mind that Akitas are naturally dog-aggres-

HOME WITH THE MANGE

Many young dogs suffer from demodectic mange, sometimes called red mange. While all breeds of dog have suffered from demodectic mange, short-coated breeds are at a greater risk. The mange manifests itself as localized infections on the face, muzzle, neck and limbs. The symptoms include hair loss and red, scaly skin. Vets routinely treat demodectic mange so that secondary infections are avoided. Many breeders remove known carriers from their programs.

Part of the social-
isation process
includes grooming
the coat. The
grooming process,
including clipping
the nails, cleaning
the ears and eyes,
as well as comb-
ing and brushing,
should be proto-
cols started while
the Akita is still a
very young puppy.

sive and may not get along with your neighbor's Pug from the very start. This will help him become well adjusted as he grows up and less prone to being timid or fearful of the new things he will encounter. Your pup's socialization began with the breeder but

PUP MEETS WORLD

Thorough socialization includes not only meeting new people but also being introduced to new experiences such as riding in the car, having his coat brushed, hearing the television, walking in a crowd—the list is endless. The more your pup experiences, and the more positive the experiences are, the less of a shock and the less frightening it will be for your pup to encounter new things.

now it is your responsibility to continue it. The socialization he receives up until the age of 12 weeks is the most critical, as this is the time when he forms his impressions of the outside world. Be especially careful during the eight-to-ten-week period, also known as the fear period. The interaction he receives during this time should be gentle and reassuring. Lack of socialization can manifest itself in fear and aggression as the dog grows up. He needs lots of human contact, affection, handling and exposure to other animals.

Once your pup has received his necessary vaccinations, feel free to take him out and about (on his lead, of course). Walk him around the neighborhood, take him on your daily errands, let people pet him, let him meet other dogs and pets, etc. Puppies do not have to try to make friends; there will be no shortage of people who will want to introduce themselves. Just make sure that you carefully supervise each meeting. If the neighborhood children want to say hello, for example, that is great—children and pups most often make great companions. Sometimes an excited child can unintentionally handle a pup too roughly, or an overzealous pup can playfully nip a little too hard. You want to make socialization experiences positive ones. What a pup learns during this very formative stage will affect his attitude toward future encounters. You want your dog to be comfortable around everyone. A pup that has a bad experience with a child may grow up to be a dog that is shy around or aggressive toward children, which is completely unacceptable with a dog as powerful and dominant as an Akita.

CONSISTENCY IN TRAINING

Dogs, being pack animals, naturally need a leader, or else they try to establish dominance in their packs. When you welcome a dog into your family, the choice of who becomes the leader and who becomes the "pack" is entirely up to you! Your pup's intuitive quest for dominance, coupled with the fact that it is nearly impossible to look at an adorable "baby wolf" Akita pup and not cave in, give the pup almost an unfair advantage in getting the upper hand! A pup will definitely test the waters to see what he can and cannot do. Do not give in to those pleading eyes—stand your ground when it comes to disciplining the pup and make sure that all family members do the same. Avoid discrepancies by having all members of the household decide on the rules before the pup even comes home...and be consistent in enforcing them! Early training shapes the dog's personality, so you cannot be unclear in what you expect.

FEAR AGGRESSION

Pups who are subjected to physical abuse during training commonly end up with behavioral problems as adults. One common result of abuse is fear aggression, in which a dog will lash out, bare his teeth, snarl and finally bite someone by whom he feels threatened. For example, your daughter may be playing with the dog one afternoon. As they play hide-and-seek, she backs the dog into a corner and, as she attempts to tease him playfully, he bites her hand. Examine the cause of this behavior. Did your daughter ever hit the dog? Did someone who resembles your daughter hit or scream at the dog?

Fortunately, fear aggression is relatively easy to correct. Have your daughter engage in only positive activities with the dog, such as feeding, petting and walking. She should not give any corrections or negative feedback. If the dog still growls or cowers away from her, allow someone else to accompany them. After approximately one week, the dog should feel that he can rely on her for many positive things, and he will also be prevented from reacting fearfully towards anyone who might resemble her.

COMMON PUPPY PROBLEMS

The best way to prevent puppy problems is to be proactive in stopping an undesirable behavior as soon as it starts. The old saying

Then replace your finger with an appropriate chew toy. While this behavior is merely annoying when the dog is young, it can become dangerous as your Akita's adult teeth grow in and his jaws develop, and he continues to think it is okay to gnaw on human appendages. Your Akita does not mean any harm with a friendly nip, but he has to learn to respect his master and never to use his jaws when playing.

CRYING/WHINING

Your pup will often cry, whine, whimper, howl or make some type of commotion when he is left alone. This is basically his way of calling out for attention to make sure that you know he is there and that you have not forgotten about him. He feels insecure when he is left alone,

Ah, sweet bribery! In canine lingo, there is no crime in a tasty bribe.

"You can't teach an old dog new tricks" does not necessarily hold true, but it is true that it is much easier to discourage bad behavior in a young developing pup than to wait until the pup's bad behavior becomes the adult dog's bad habit. There are some problems that are especially prevalent in puppies as they develop.

NIPPING

As puppies start to teethe, they feel the need to sink their teeth into anything available...unfortunately that includes your fingers, arms, hair and toes. You may find this behavior cute for the first *five seconds*...until you feel just how sharp those puppy teeth are. This is something you want to discourage immediately and consistently with a firm "No!"

PUPPY PROBLEMS
The majority of problems that are commonly seen in young pups will disappear as your dog gets older. However, how you deal with problems when he is young will determine how he reacts to discipline as an adult dog. It is important to establish who is boss (ideally it will be you!) right away when you are first bonding with your dog. This bond will set the tone for the rest of your life together.

when you are out of the house and he is in his crate or when you are in another part of the house and he cannot see you. The noise he is making is an expression of the anxiety he feels at being alone, so he needs to be taught that being alone is okay. You are not actually training the dog to stop making noise, you are training him to feel comfortable when he is alone and thus removing the need for him to make the noise. This is where the crate with cozy bedding and a toy comes in handy. You want to know that he is safe when you are not there to supervise, and you know that he will be safe in his crate rather than roaming freely about the house. In order for the pup to stay in his crate without making a fuss, he needs to be comfortable in his crate. On that note, it is extremely important that the crate is never used as a form of punishment, or the pup will have a negative association with the crate.

Accustom the pup to the crate in short, gradually increasing time intervals in which you put him in the crate, maybe with a treat, and stay in the room with him. If he cries or makes a fuss, do not go to him, but stay in his sight. Gradually he will realize that staying in his crate is okay without your help, and it will not be so traumatic for him when you are not around. You may

CHEWING TIPS

Chewing goes hand in hand with nipping in the sense that a teething puppy is always looking for a way to soothe his aching gums. In this case, instead of chewing on you, he may have taken a liking to your favorite shoe or something else that he should not be chewing. Again, realize that this is a normal canine behavior that does not need to be discouraged, only redirected. Your pup just needs to be taught what is acceptable to chew on and what is off-limits. Consistently tell him "No!" when you catch him chewing on something forbidden and give him a chew toy.

Conversely, praise him when you catch him chewing on something appropriate. In this way, you are discouraging the inappropriate behavior and reinforcing the desired behavior. The puppy's chewing should stop after his adult teeth have come in, but an adult dog continues to chew for various reasons—perhaps because he is bored, needs to relieve tension or just likes to chew. That is why it is important to redirect his chewing when he is still young.

want to leave the radio on softly when you leave the house; the sound of human voices may be comforting to him.

AKITA

FEEDING YOUR AKITA

Akita pups should be kept on a good whole-food diet consisting of raw meat and bones and, if need be, a good puppy dry food. He should never be given cooked bones, as they become brittle with cooking. He can be switched to adult food at about six months of age, but if he is fed raw beef and chicken bones, he will get enough calcium and can get by quite nicely on adult dry food as a filler. There are many good-quality dry foods on the market. Your breeder can recommend one upon which he has relied with success for the Akita.

There is much enlightenment all over the world as regards both

The choice of how and what to feed your Akita puppy is your own. Discuss the options with your breeder.

FEEDING TIPS
- Dog food must be served at room temperature, neither too hot nor too cold. Fresh water, changed often and served in a clean bowl, is mandatory, especially when feeding dry food.
- Never feed your dog from the table while you are eating, and never feed your dog leftovers from your own meal. They usually contain too much fat and too much seasoning.
- Dogs must chew their food. Hard pellets are excellent; soups and stews are to be avoided.
- Don't add leftovers or any extras to commercial dog food. The normal food is usually balanced, and adding something extra destroys the balance.
- Except for age-related changes, dogs do not require dietary variations. They can be fed the same diet, day after day, without their becoming bored or ill.

human and pet diets. That which comes from a box or sack is never a complete food. You would surely not feed your child cereal and nothing more for his lifetime. Why would you do that to your dog? Cereals and dry food are fine, but only when there are no fresh fruit, vegetables and, in the case of your Akita, raw meat.

The subject of natural food is a complex one just now being explored by a public that has been too busy to prepare wholesome food and quite willing to let the food companies do it for them, as well as brain-washed into believing that the contents of a package, so full of preservatives that it has a shelf life of several years, could possibly be life-sustaining when eaten.

WATER

Just as your dog needs proper nutrition from his food, water is an essential "nutrient" as well. Water keeps the dog's body properly hydrated and promotes normal function of the body's systems. During house-training it is necessary to keep an eye on how much water your Akita is drinking, but once he is reliably trained he should have access to clean fresh water at all times, especially if you feed dry food. Make certain that the dog's water bowl is clean, and change the water often.

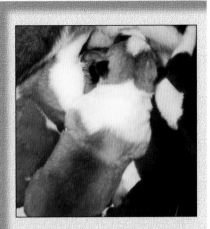

"NURSING" TO HEALTH

Puppies instinctively want to suck milk from their mother's teats and a normal puppy will exhibit this behavior from just a few moments following birth. If puppies do not attempt to suckle within the first half-hour or so, they should be encouraged to do so by placing them on the nipples, having selected ones with plenty of milk. This early milk supply is important in providing colostrum to protect the puppies during the first eight to ten weeks of their lives. Although a mother's milk is much better than any milk formula, despite there being some excellent ones available, if the puppies do not feed, you will have to feed them yourself. For those with less experience, advice from a veterinarian is important so that you feed not only the right quantity of milk but that of correct quality, fed at suitably frequent intervals, usually every two hours during the first few days of life.

DRINK, DRANK, DRUNK— MAKE IT A DOUBLE

In both humans and dogs, as well as other living organisms, water forms the major part of nearly every body tissue. Naturally, we take water for granted, but without it, life as we know it would cease.

For dogs, water is needed to keep their bodies functioning biochemically. Additionally, water is needed to replace the water lost while panting. Unlike humans, who are able to sweat to dissipate heat, dogs must pant to cool down, thereby losing the vital water that their bodies need to regulate their body temperatures. Humans lose electrolyte-containing products and other body-fluid components through sweating; dogs do not lose anything except water.

Water is essential always, but especially so when the weather is hot or humid or when your dog is exercising or working vigorously.

EXERCISE

Akitas need exercise. Being mentally and physically active, such as jogging around the park or walking around the neighborhood, stimulates the mind and body. Akitas are not ball-chasers, nor are they hyperactive, but some form of exercise that makes the dog pant (sweat) every day is important.

Puppies should be allowed to romp and play just like children. Your young child would not be allowed to play with the adult football team and, likewise, your juvenile dog should not be allowed to engage in rough play with older dogs. Strenuous exercise in any form should be avoided until soft tendons and bones have finished developing.

Knee injuries are common in large-breed puppies and in large-breed adults that are allowed to engage in activities for which they are ill-suited. Even the most perfectly conditioned athletes suffer such injuries, so it is only common sense that undeveloped pups and unconditioned adult dogs are accidents (and injuries) waiting to happen.

GROOMING

Grooming the Akita's coat is not difficult, but it does require regular attention. Thorough combing and brushing should be done at least twice a week, taking care to remove all loose hair from the coat. The Akita will usually cast his coat twice a year. During this time, he will need grooming every day to keep up with the great hair loss. There will be an enormous amount of undercoat in a properly coated dog, and this will need to be pulled out with a special rake-like tool designed for that purpose.

We would recommend a good warm bath at the beginning of the shedding process, as this loosens the coat, thus enabling you to remove dead hair more speedily. If the undercoat is not removed, it will cause skin irritation that can lead to ongoing skin problems. Although the Akita's coat is too harsh to mat and tangle, as will the coats of other double-coated breeds, it is important to remove dead hair on a regular basis and never let the coat become stuck together with dead hair.

Coat length and density can vary tremendously. The "long coats" probably came from the Chow Chow, and although not accepted in the show ring, they make wonderfully impressive pets. Mrs. Andrews has been a great fan of the "long coats" as pets and recognizes these special dogs' place in Akita history. Long-coated "Akita-type" dogs known as Karafuto were used in the famous Japanese Polar expedition and, although they had to be abandoned, many survived

THE CANINE GOURMET
Your dog does not prefer a fresh bone. Indeed, he wants it properly aged and, if given such a treat indoors, he is more likely to try to bury it in the carpet than he is to settle in for a good chew! If you have a garden, give him such delicacies outside and guide him to a place suitable for his "bone yard." He will carefully place the treasure in its earthy vault and seemingly forget about it. Trust me, his seeming distaste or lack of thanks for your thoughtfulness is not that at all. He will return in a few days to inspect the bone, perhaps to re-bury it, and when it is just right, he will relish it as much as you do that cooked-to-perfection steak. If he is in a concrete or bricked kennel run, he will be especially frustrated at the hopelessness of the situation. He will vacillate between ignoring it completely, giving it a few licks to speed the curing process with saliva, and trying to hide it behind the water bowl! When the bone has aged a bit, he will set to work on it.

A Worthy Investment

Veterinary studies have proven that a balanced high-quality diet pays off in your dog's coat quality, behavior and activity level. Invest in premium brands for the maximum payoff with your dog.

the extreme winter and greeted returning mushers with enthusiasm.

Long-coated Akitas can mat and will require combing out more often simply due to the softness, extra length and fullness of the coat. Make certain that the dog is dry to the skin, as dampness left in the coat can lead to the development of eczema, which is an uncomfortable skin irritation like a heat rash. Dampness under the throat,

on the chest or on the back where the tail rests can often lead to what are commonly called "hot spots."

With either coat type, it is also advisable to bathe again at the end of the shedding period as it will speed up the reappearance of a new, healthy, shiny coat with vibrant color. Oddly, as the coat begins to die out, the color will become pale and dull. The loss of thick hair on the legs can also make your Akita appear to be "fine-boned," and shedding also can detract from his big full "bottle-brush" tail.

BATHING AND DRYING

When bathing, be sure to use a gentle shampoo that will not cause irritation, taking extreme care in rinsing thoroughly all shampoo from the coat. Do remember to insert cotton balls into the ears to protect them from the water (and to remove them afterwards). Be very careful when bathing the head, so as not to allow any soap or water to get into the eyes. In fact, a tearless "baby" shampoo is an excellent choice for washing the head. Even with the cotton ball in the ears, be very careful when rinsing or you will cause the dog to shake violently if water trickles into the ear canal—and you will have been rinsed as well! Wearing a waterproof apron or rain gear is a good idea.

"DOES THIS COLLAR MAKE ME LOOK FAT?"

While humans may obsess about how they look and how trim their bodies are, many people believe that extra weight on their dogs is a good thing. The truth is, pets should not be over- or under-weight, as both can lead to or signal sickness. In order to tell how fit your pet is, run your hands over his ribs. Are his ribs buried under a layer of fat or are they sticking out considerably? If your pet is within his normal weight range, you should be able to feel the ribs easily, but they should not protrude abnormally. If you stand above him, the outline of his body should resemble an hourglass. Some breeds do tend to be leaner while some are a bit stockier, but making sure your dog is the right weight for his breed will certainly contribute to his good health.

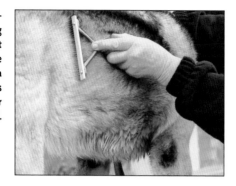

The rake is effective for removing dead undercoat hair. Hold the rake in such a manner that it is comfortable for your hand.

The grooming table should be at a comfortable height so you can clearly see what you are doing. Don't forget that magnificent tail.

The Akita will require more regular brushing during the bi-annual shedding periods. A patient and handsome Akita stands while author Meg Purnell-Carpenter grooms.

After bathing, we recommend that you dry your Akita with a blow dryer (set on "low"). This will not only dry the coat right down to the skin but it also will blast dead and unwanted coat away. Using a pin brush, you should lift and separate the coat as you work through it with the hair dryer so that each hair is thoroughly dry. This too will speed the drying process and help to train the coat to stand up and away from the body, as is proper for the breed. When finished, dry brush the coat thoroughly, remembering that you should lift the Akita's coat and make it stand off the body while brushing.

EARS, TEETH AND TOENAILS

Remember to check all parts of the dog's body when grooming. Any signs of fleas or other parasites will become evident and can be attended to. The ears should be cleaned regularly with a tissue or damp cloth. Teeth should be checked for any redness around the gum area or signs of plaque or decay, and should be cleaned if necessary. There are special toothbrushes and flavored toothpastes made for dogs, which make this job easier. A good knucklebone from your local butcher shop will also serve to keep your Akita's teeth clean, while providing soothing chewing exercise and enjoyment for your dog. Always keep a close eye on your Akita whenever he is chewing on a bone.

Keep toenails trimmed so as to keep the feet healthy and the toes nice and tight. You can either trim them yourself or ask your veterinarian or groomer to perform this task for you. If you trim the toenails yourself, take great care to never trim them so close as to cut the quick. Making the dog bleed will cause him to forever resent having his feet handled.

The quick is a blood vessel that runs through the center of each nail and grows rather close to the end. It will bleed if cut, which will be quite painful for the dog as it contains nerve

GROOMING EQUIPMENT

Always purchase the best quality grooming equipment so that your tools will last for many years to come. Here are some basics:

- Pin brush
- Metal comb
- Scissors
- Rubber mat
- Dog shampoo
- Spray hose attachment
- Towels
- Blow dryer
- Ear cleaner
- Cotton balls
- Nail clippers
- Dental-care products

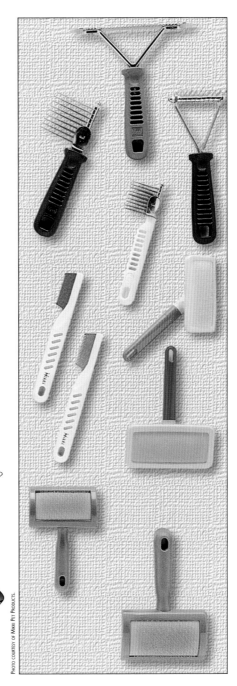

Your local pet shop should have a complete array of grooming tools so you may select the tools with which you can properly groom your Akita.

PHOTO COURTESY OF MIKKI PET PRODUCTS.

Nail Maintenance

Nail Casing
Quick

Cut Line

Dark-Colored Nails

With black or dark nails, where the quick is not easy to see, it's best to clip only the tip of the nail or to use a file.

Light-Colored Nails

In light-colored nails, clipping is much simpler because you can see the vein (or quick) that grows inside the casing.

endings. Keep some type of clotting agent on hand, such as a styptic pencil or styptic powder (the type used for shaving). This will stop the bleeding quickly when applied to the end of the cut nail. Do not panic if you cut

BATHING BEAUTY

Once you are sure that the dog is thoroughly rinsed, squeeze the excess water out of his coat with your hand and dry him with an heavy towel. You may choose to use a blow dryer on his coat or just let it dry naturally. In cold weather, never allow your dog outside with a wet coat.

There are "dry bath" products on the market, which are sprays and powders intended for spot cleaning, that can be used between regular baths if necessary. They are not substitutes for regular baths, but they are easy to use for touch-ups as they do not require rinsing.

SOAP IT UP

The use of human soap products like shampoo, bubble bath and hand soap can be damaging to a dog's coat and skin. Human products are too strong; they remove the protective oils coating the dog's hair and skin that make him water-resistant. Use only shampoo made especially for dogs. You may like to use a medicated shampoo, which will help to keep external parasites at bay.

the quick, just stop the bleeding and talk soothingly to your dog. Once he has calmed down, move on to the next nail. It is better to clip a little at a time, particularly with black-nailed dogs.

If you are unable to perform these basic requirements or do not have the time or bathing facilities, use a professional groomer on a regular basis. Do remember to book the appointment in advance and acquaint the Akita with his new "beautician" at an early age. In fact, it will do him good to be left at the grooming shop or kennel for a few hours so that he becomes more confident and self-assured. Dogs that are never taken anywhere or that have never been separated from their family can become stressed when a family emergency or vacation forces the first stay away from home.

Preparation for the show ring will involve far more detail and dedication. We recommend that you take advice from your breeder or fellow breed club members. Ideally, every Akita should be well cared for and should look like the glamorous dogs seen on television.

TRAVELING WITH YOUR DOG

CAR TRAVEL

You should accustom your Akita to riding in a car at an early age.

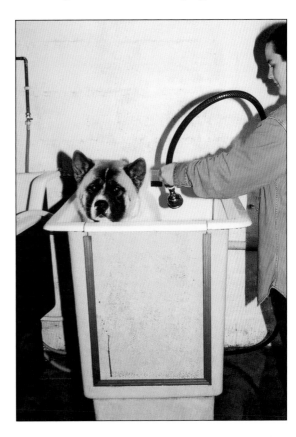

A visit to the grooming salon may be the perfect way to give your Akita his occasional bath!

You may or may not take him in the car often, but at the very least he will need to go to the vet and you do not want these trips to be traumatic for the dog or troublesome for you. The safest

PEDICURE TIP

A dog that spends a lot of time outside on a hard surface, such as cement or pavement, will have his nails naturally worn down and may not need to have them trimmed as often, except maybe in the colder months when he is not outside as much. Regardless, it is best to get your dog accustomed to the nail-trimming procedure at an early age so that he is used to it. Some dogs are especially sensitive about having their feet touched, but if a dog has experienced it since puppyhood, it should not bother him.

way for a dog to ride in the car is in his crate. If he uses a crate in the house, you can use the same crate for travel. Of course, an Akita's giant crate requires an equally giant vehicle. If you cannot fit the dog's crate in your vehicle, you might consider a harness, which works like a seat belt, or a safety gate.

If you are fortunate to have a sports utility vehicle or van, you can use the crate, which is by far the safest method. Put the pup in the crate and see how he reacts. If you have crate-trained the pup (as you should have), you will have no problem with the pup in your SUV. Do not let the dog roam loose in the vehicle—this is very dangerous! If you should stop short, your dog can be thrown and injured. If the dog starts climbing on you and pestering you while you are driving, you will not be able to concentrate on the road. It is an unsafe situation for everyone—human and canine.

For long trips, be prepared to stop to let the dog relieve himself. Take with you whatever you need to clean up after him, including some paper kitchen towels and perhaps some old toweling for use should he have an accident in the car or suffer from motion sickness.

AIR TRAVEL
Contact your chosen airline before proceeding with your

Accustom the puppy to your vehicle at a young age. Use the dog's crate or a safety gate to transport your Akita.

Select a boarding kennel close to your home that has facilities large enough for your Akita. Check out the cleanliness, the staff and the costs before you actually need the facility.

travel plans that include your Akita. The dog will be required to travel in a fiberglass crate and you should always check in advance with the airline regarding specific requirements. To help put the dog at ease, give

DEADLY DECAY

Did you know that periodontal disease (a condition of the bone and gums surrounding a tooth) can be fatal? Having your dog's teeth and mouth checked yearly can prevent it.

him one of his favorite toys in the crate. Do not feed the dog for at least six hours before the trip in order to minimize his need to relieve himself. However, certain regulations specify that water must always be made available to the dog in the crate.

Make sure your dog is properly identified and that your contact information appears on his ID tags and on his crate. Animals travel in a different area of the plane than human passengers, so every rule must be strictly followed so as to prevent the risk of getting separated from your dog.

VACATIONS AND BOARDING
So you want to take a family vacation—and you want to include *all* members of the family. You would probably

"Who's afraid of the big bad wolf?" *Some staff members at boarding kennels.* Choose your facility with care.

make arrangements for accommodations ahead of time anyway, but this is especially important when traveling with a dog. You do not want to make an overnight stop at the only place around for miles and find out that they do not allow dogs. Also, you do not want to reserve a place for your family without confirming that you are traveling with a dog because if it is against their policy you may not have a place to stay.

Alternatively, if you are traveling and choose not to bring your Akita, you will have to make arrangements for him while you are away. Some options are to take him to a neighbor's house to stay while you are gone, to have a trusted neighbor stop by often or stay at your house or to bring your dog

IDENTIFICATION OPTIONS

As puppies become more and more expensive, especially those puppies of high quality for showing and/or breeding, they have a greater chance of being stolen. The usual collar dog tag is, of course, easily removed. But there are two more permanent techniques that have become widely used for identification.

The puppy microchip implantation involves the injection of a small microchip, about the size of a corn kernel, under the skin of the dog. If your dog shows up at a clinic or shelter, or is offered for resale under less-than-savory circumstances, it can be positively identified by the microchip. The microchip is scanned, and a registry quickly identifies you as the owner.

Tattooing is done on various parts of the dog, from his belly to his ears. The number tattooed can be your telephone number, your dog's registration number or any other number that you can easily memorize. When professional dog thieves see a tattooed dog, they usually lose interest. For the safety of our dogs, no laboratory facility or dog broker will accept a tattooed dog as stock.

Discuss microchipping and tattooing with your veterinarian and breeder. Some vets perform these services on their own premises for a reasonable fee. To ensure that your dog's identification is effective, be certain that the dog is then properly registered with a legitimate national database.

to a reputable boarding kennel. If you choose to board him at a kennel, you should visit in advance to see the facilities provided, how clean they are and where the dogs are kept. Talk to some of the employees and see how they treat the dogs—do they spend time with the dogs, play with them, exercise them, etc.? Also find out the kennel's policy on vaccinations and what they require. This is for all of the dogs' safety, since when dogs are kept together, there is a greater risk of diseases being passed from dog to dog.

IDENTIFICATION

Your Akita is your valued companion and friend. That is why you always keep a close eye on him and you have made sure that he cannot escape from the yard or wriggle out of his collar and run away from you. However, accidents can happen and there may come a time when your dog unexpectedly gets separated from you. If your Akita has escaped his collar, then some other form of identification will be necessary since he will not have his ID tag with him! Therefore, in addition to the ID tag, you should consider a tattoo or a microchip to increase the chances of his being returned to you safely and quickly.

TRAINING YOUR
AKITA

Living with an untrained dog is a lot like owning a piano that you do not know how to play—it is a nice object to look at but it does not do much more than that to bring you pleasure. Now try taking piano lessons and suddenly the piano comes alive and brings forth magical sounds and rhythms that set your heart singing and your body swaying.

The same is true with your Akita. Any dog is a big responsibility and if not trained sensibly may develop unacceptable behavior that annoys you or could even cause family friction.

To train your Akita, you may like to enroll in an obedience class. Teach him good manners as you learn how and why he behaves the way he does. Find out how to communicate with your dog and how to recognize and understand his communications with you. Suddenly the dog takes on a new role in your life—

Approach your Akita's education with patirnce and consistency. Your puppy will accept your authority if you treat him fairly.

THE GOLDEN RULE

The golden rule of dog training is simple. For each "question" (command), there is only one correct answer (reaction). One command = one reaction. Keep practicing the command until the dog reacts correctly without hesitating. Be repetitive but not monotonous. Dogs get bored just as people do!

PARENTAL GUIDANCE

Training a dog is a life experience. Many parents admit that much of what they know about raising children they learned from caring for their dogs. Dogs respond to love, fairness and guidance, just as children do. Become a good dog owner and you may become an even better parent.

he is clever, interesting, well-behaved and fun to be with. He demonstrates his bond of devotion to you daily. In other words, your Akita does wonders for your ego because he constantly reminds you that you are not only his leader, you are his hero!

Those involved with teaching dog obedience and counseling owners about their dogs' behavior have discovered some interesting facts about dog ownership. For example, training dogs when they are puppies results in the highest rate of success in developing well-mannered and well-adjusted adult dogs. Training an older dog, from six months to six years of age, can produce almost equal results providing that the owner accepts the dog's slower rate of learning capability and is willing to work patiently to help the dog succeed at developing to his fullest potential. Unfortunately, many owners of untrained adult dogs lack the patience factor, so they do not persist until their dogs are successful at learning particular behaviors.

Training a puppy aged 10 to 16 weeks (20 weeks at the most) is like working with a dry sponge in a pool of water. The pup soaks up whatever you show him and constantly looks for more things to do and learn. At this early age, his body is not yet producing hormones, and therein lies the reason for such a high rate of success. Without hormones, he is focused on his owners and not particularly interested in investigating other places, dogs, people, etc. You are his leader: his provider of food, water, shelter and security. He latches onto you and wants to stay close. He will usually follow you from room to room, will not let you out of his sight when you are outdoors with him and will respond in like manner to the people and animals you encounter. If you greet a friend warmly, he will be happy to greet the person as well. If, however, you are hesitant, even anxious, about the approach of a stranger, he will respond accordingly.

Once the puppy begins to produce hormones, his natural curiosity emerges and he begins to investigate the world around him. It is at this time when you may notice that the untrained dog begins to wander away from you and even ignore your commands to stay close. When this behavior becomes a problem, the owner has two choices: get rid of the dog or train him. It is strongly urged that you choose the latter option.

There are usually classes within a reasonable distance from the owner's home, but you can also do a lot to train your dog yourself. Sometimes there are classes available, but the tuition is too costly. Whatever the

REAP THE REWARDS
If you start with a normal, healthy dog and give him time, patience and some carefully executed lessons, you will reap the rewards of that training for the life of the dog. And what a life it will be! The two of you will find immeasurable pleasure in the companionship you have built together with love, respect and understanding.

methods of teaching and the techniques we use in training basic behaviors are the same. After all, no dog, whether puppy or adult, likes harsh or inhumane methods. All creatures, however, respond favorably to gentle motivational methods and sincere praise and encouragement. Now let us get started.

HOUSE-TRAINING

You can train a puppy to relieve himself wherever you choose, but this must be somewhere suitable. You should bear in mind from the outset that when your puppy is old enough to go out in public places, any canine droppings must be removed at once. You will always have to carry with you a plastic bag or "pooper-scooper."

Outdoor training includes such surfaces as grass, soil and cement. Indoor training usually means training your dog to newspaper. When deciding on the surface and location that you will

MEALTIME
Mealtime should be a peaceful time for your puppy. Do not put his food and water bowls in a high-traffic area in the house. For example, give him his own little corner of the kitchen where he can eat undisturbed and where he will not be underfoot. Do not allow small children or other family members to disturb the pup when he is eating.

circumstances, the solution to training your Akita without professional assistance or formal training classes lies within the pages of this book.

This chapter is devoted to helping you train your Akita at home. If the recommended procedures are followed faithfully, you may expect positive results that will prove rewarding both to you and your dog.

Whether your new charge is a puppy or a mature adult, the

THINK BEFORE YOU BARK
Dogs are sensitive to their masters' moods and emotions. Use your voice wisely when communicating with your dog. Never raise your voice at your dog unless you are trying to correct him. "Barking" at your dog can become as meaningless as "dogs-peak" is to you.

Puppies learn by watching and sniffing. Adult dogs pass along their correct behavior and habits to younger dogs.

want your Akita to use, be sure it is going to be permanent. Training your dog to grass and then changing your mind two

PAPER CAPER

Never line your pup's sleeping area with newspaper. Puppy litters are usually raised on newspaper and, once in your home, the puppy will immediately associate newspaper with voiding. Never put newspaper on any floor while house-training, as this will only confuse the puppy. If you are paper-training him, use paper in his designated relief area only. Finally, restrict water intake after evening meals. Offer a few licks at a time—never let a young puppy gulp water after meals.

months later is extremely diffi-cult for both dog and owner.

Next, choose the command you will use each and every time you want your puppy to void. "Hurry up" and "Let's go" are examples of commands commonly used by dog owners. Get in the habit of giving the puppy your chosen relief command before you take him out. That way, when he becomes an adult, you will be able to deter-mine if he wants to go out when you ask him. A confirmation will be signs of interest, such as wagging his tail, watching you intently, going to the door, etc.

PUPPY'S NEEDS

Your new puppy needs to relieve himself after play periods, after

CANINE DEVELOPMENT SCHEDULE

It is important to understand how and at what age a puppy develops into adulthood. If you are a puppy owner, consult the following Canine Development Schedule to determine the stage of development your puppy is currently experiencing. This knowledge will help you as you work with the puppy in the weeks and months ahead.

Period	Age	Characteristics
FIRST TO THIRD	BIRTH TO SEVEN WEEKS	Puppy needs food, sleep and warmth, and responds to simple and gentle touching. Needs mother for security and disciplining. Needs littermates for learning and interacting with other dogs. Pup learns to function within a pack and learns pack order of dominance. Begin socializing pup with adults and children for short periods. Pup begins to become aware of his environment.
FOURTH	EIGHT TO TWELVE WEEKS	Brain is fully developed. Pup needs socializing with outside world. Remove from mother and littermates. Needs to change from canine pack to human pack. Human dominance necessary. Fear period occurs between 8 and 12 weeks. Avoid fright and pain.
FIFTH	THIRTEEN TO SIXTEEN WEEKS	Training and formal obedience should begin. Less association with other dogs, more with people, places, situations. Period will pass easily if you remember this is pup's change-to-adolescence time. Be firm and fair. Flight instinct prominent. Permissiveness and over-disciplining can do permanent damage. Praise for good behavior.
JUVENILE	FOUR TO EIGHT MONTHS	Another fear period about 7 to 8 months of age. It passes quickly, but be cautious of fright and pain. Sexual maturity reached. Dominant traits established. Dog should understand sit, down, come and stay by now.

NOTE: THESE ARE APPROXIMATE TIME FRAMES. ALLOW FOR INDIVIDUAL DIFFERENCES IN PUPPIES.

each meal, after he has been sleeping and at any time he indicates that he is looking for a place to urinate or defecate. The urinary and intestinal tract muscles of very young puppies are not fully developed. Therefore, like human babies, puppies need to relieve themselves frequently.

Take your puppy out often—every hour for an eight-week-old, for example, and always immediately after sleeping and eating. The older the puppy, the less often he will need to relieve himself. Finally, as a mature healthy adult, he will require only three to five relief trips per day.

HOUSING

Since the types of housing and control you provide for your puppy have a direct relationship on the success of house-training, we consider the various aspects of both before we begin training.

Taking a new puppy home and turning him loose in your house can be compared to turning a child loose in a sports arena and telling the child that the place is all his! The sheer enormity of the place would be too much for him to handle.

Instead, offer the puppy clearly defined areas where he can play, sleep, eat and live. A room of the house where the family gathers is the most obvious choice. Puppies are social animals and need to feel a part of the pack right from the start. Hearing your voice, watching you while you are

PRACTICE MAKES PERFECT!
- Have training lessons with your dog every day in several short segments—three to five times a day for a few minutes at a time is ideal.
- Do not have long practice sessions. The dog will become easily bored.
- Never practice when you are tired, ill, worried or in an otherwise negative mood. This will transmit to the dog and may have an adverse effect on his performance.

Think fun, short and above all *positive!* End each session on a high note, rather than a failed exercise, and make sure to give a lot of praise. Enjoy the training and help your dog enjoy it, too.

ATTENTION!
Your dog is actually training you at the same time you are training him. Dogs do things to get attention. They usually repeat whatever succeeds in getting your attention.

doing things and smelling you nearby are all positive reinforcers that he is now a member of your pack. Usually a family room, the kitchen or a nearby adjoining breakfast area is ideal for providing safety and security for both puppy and owner.

Within that room there should be a smaller area that the puppy can call his own. An alcove, a wire dog crate or a gated corner from which he can view the activities of his new family will be fine. The size of the area or crate is the key factor here. The area must be large enough for the puppy to lie down and stretch out as well as stand up without rubbing his head on the top, yet small enough so that he cannot relieve himself at one end and sleep at the other without coming into contact with his droppings until fully trained to relieve himself outside. The designated area should contain clean bedding and a toy. Water must always be available, in a non-spill container.

Dogs are, by nature, clean animals and will not remain close to their relief areas unless forced to do so. In those cases, they then become dirty dogs and usually remain that way for life.

CONTROL
By *control*, we mean helping the puppy to create a lifestyle pattern that will be compatible to that of his human pack (*you*!). Just as we guide little children to learn our way of life, we must show the puppy when it is time to play, eat, sleep, exercise and even entertain himself.

Your puppy should always sleep in his crate. He should also learn that, during times of household confusion and excessive human activity such as at breakfast when family members are preparing for the day, he can play by himself in relative safety and comfort in his designated area. Each time you leave the puppy alone, he should understand exactly where he is to stay. Puppies are chewers. They cannot tell the difference between bones, lamp cords, television wires, shoes, table legs, etc. Chewing into a television wire, for example, can be fatal to the puppy while a shorted wire can start a fire in the house.

If the puppy chews on the arm of the chair when he is alone, you will probably discipline him angrily when you get home. Thus, he makes the association that your coming home means he is going to be punished. (He will not remember chewing the chair and is incapable of making the association of the discipline with his naughty deed.)

Other times of excitement, such as family parties, holidays, etc., can be fun for the puppy providing he can view the activities from the security of his designated area. He is not underfoot and he is not being fed all sorts of tidbits that will probably cause him stomach distress, yet he still feels a part of the fun.

SCHEDULE
A puppy should be taken to his relief area each time he is released from his designated area, after a meal, after a play session and when he first awakens in the morning (at age eight weeks, this can mean 5 a.m.!). The puppy will indicate that he's ready "to go" by circling or sniffing busily—do not misinterpret these signs. For a puppy less than ten weeks of age, a routine of taking him out every hour is necessary. As the puppy grows, he will be able to wait for longer periods of time.

Keep trips to his relief area short. Stay no more than five or six minutes and then return to the house. If he goes during that time, praise him lavishly and take him indoors immediately. If he does not, but he has an accident when you go back indoors, pick him up immediately, say "No!" and return to his relief area. Wait a few minutes, then return to the house again. Never hit a puppy or put his face in urine or excrement when he has had an accident!

Once indoors, put the puppy in his crate until you have had time to clean up his accident. Then release him to the family area and watch him more closely

TAKE THE LEAD
Do not carry your dog to his relief area. Lead him there on a leash or, better yet, encourage him to follow you to the spot. If you start carrying him to his spot, you might end up doing this routine forever and your dog will have the satisfaction of having trained *you*.

THE SUCCESS METHOD

Success that comes by luck is usually short-lived. Success that comes by well-thought-out proven methods is often more easily achieved and permanent. This is the Success Method. It is designed to give you, the puppy owner, a simple yet proven way to help your puppy develop clean living habits and a feeling of security in his new environment.

6 Steps to Successful Crate Training

1 Tell the puppy "Crate time!" and place him in the crate with a small treat (a piece of cheese or half of a biscuit). Let him stay in the crate for five minutes while you are in the same room. Then release him and praise lavishly. Never release him when he is fussing. Wait until he is quiet before you let him out.

2 Repeat Step 1 several times a day.

3 The next day, place the puppy in the crate as before. Let him stay there for ten minutes. Do this several times.

4 Continue building time in five-minute increments until the puppy stays in his crate for 30 minutes with you in the room. Always take him to his relief area after prolonged periods in his crate.

5 Now go back to Step 1 and let the puppy stay in his crate for five minutes, this time while you are out of the room.

6 Once again, build crate time in five-minute increments with you out of the room. When the puppy will stay willingly in his crate (he may even fall asleep!) for 30 minutes with you out of the room, he will be ready to stay in it for several hours at a time.

than before. Chances are, his accident was a result of your not picking up his signal or waiting too long before offering him the opportunity to relieve himself. Never hold a grudge against the puppy for accidents.

Let the puppy learn that going outdoors means it is time to relieve himself, not play. Once trained, he will be able to play indoors and out and still differ-

HOW MANY TIMES A DAY?

AGE	RELIEF TRIPS
To 14 weeks	10
14–22 weeks	8
22–32 weeks	6
Adulthood (dog stops growing)	4

These are estimates, of course, but they are a guide to the *minimum* number of opportunities a dog should have each day to relieve himself.

entiate between the times for play versus the times for relief.

Help him develop regular hours for naps, being alone, playing by himself and just resting, all in his crate. Encourage him to entertain himself while you are busy with your activities. Let him learn that having you near is comforting, but it is not your main purpose in life to provide him with undivided attention.

Each time you put a puppy in his own area, use the same command, whatever suits best. Soon he will run to his crate or special area when he hears you say those words.

Crate training provides safety for you, the puppy and the home.

Practice at home with your budding show dog. Make training time a part of your Akita's structured routine.

It also provides the puppy with a feeling of security, and that helps the puppy achieve self-confidence and clean habits. Remember that one of the primary ingredients in house-training your puppy is control. Regardless of your lifestyle, there will always be occasions when you will need to have a place where your dog can stay and be happy and safe. Crate training is the answer for now and in the future.

In conclusion, a few key elements are really all you need for a successful house-training method—consistency, frequency, praise, control and supervision. By following these procedures with a normal, healthy puppy, you and the puppy will soon be past the stage of accidents and ready to move on to a clean and rewarding life together.

ROLES OF DISCIPLINE, REWARD AND PUNISHMENT

Discipline, training one to act in accordance with rules, brings order to life. It is as simple as that. Without discipline, particularly in a group society, chaos reigns supreme and the group will eventually perish. Humans and canines are social animals and need some form of discipline in order to function effectively. They must procure food, protect their home base and reproduce to keep the species going. If there were no discipline in the lives of social animals, they would eventually die from starvation and/or predation by other stronger animals.

In the case of domestic canines, dogs need discipline in their lives in order to understand how their pack (you and other family members) functions and how they must act in order to survive.

A large humane society in a highly populated area recently surveyed dog owners regarding their satisfaction with their relationships with their dogs. People who had trained their dogs were 75% more satisfied with their pets than those who had never trained their dogs.

Dr. Edward Thorndike, a well-known psychologist, established *Thorndike's Theory of Learning*, which states that a behavior that results in a pleasant event tends to be repeated. Likewise, a behav-

CALM DOWN

Dogs will do anything for your attention. If you reward the dog when he is calm and attentive, you will develop a well-mannered dog. If, on the other hand, you greet your dog excitedly and encourage him to wrestle with you, the dog will greet you the same way and you will have a hyperactive dog on your hands.

ior that results in an unpleasant event tends not to be repeated. It is this theory on which training methods are based today. For example, if you manipulate a dog to perform a specific behavior and reward him for doing it, he is likely to do it again because he enjoyed the end result.

Occasionally, punishment, a penalty inflicted for an offense, is necessary. The best type of punishment often comes from an outside source. For example, a child is told not to touch the stove because he may get burned. He disobeys and touches the stove. In doing so, he receives a burn. From that time on, he respects the heat of the stove and avoids contact with it. Therefore, a behavior that results in an unpleasant event tends not to be repeated.

A good example of a dog learning the hard way is the dog who chases the house cat. He is told many times to leave the cat alone, yet he persists in teasing the cat. Then, one day he begins chasing the cat but the cat turns and swipes a claw across the dog's face, leaving him with a painful gash on his nose. The final result is that the dog stops chasing the cat.

Akitas do not tolerate endless repetition of commands. Be precise and be brief and your Akita will respond most favorably.

TRAINING EQUIPMENT

COLLAR AND LEAD

For an Akita, the collar and lead that you use for training must be one with which you are easily able to work, the right size for the dog and perfectly safe.

TREATS

Have a bag of treats on hand. Something nutritious and easy to swallow works best. Use a soft treat, a chunk of cheese or a piece of cooked chicken rather than a dry biscuit. By the time the dog has finished chewing a dry treat, he will forget why he is being rewarded in the first place! In training, rewarding the dog with a food treat will help him associate praise and the treats with learning new behaviors that obviously please his owner. Using food rewards, by the way, will not teach a dog to beg at the table—the only way to teach a dog to beg

TRAINING RULES

If you want to be successful in training your dog, you have four rules to obey yourself:
1. Develop an understanding of how a dog thinks.
2. Do not blame the dog for lack of communication.
3. Define your dog's personality and act accordingly.
4. Have patience and be consistent.

at the table is to give him food from the table.

TRAINING BEGINS: ASK THE DOG A QUESTION

In order to teach your dog anything, you must first get his attention. After all, he cannot learn anything if he is looking away from you with his mind on something else.

To get his attention, ask him "School?" and immediately walk over to him and give him a treat as you tell him "Good dog." Wait a minute or two and repeat the routine, this time with a treat in your hand as you approach within a foot of the dog. Do not go directly to him, but stop about a foot short of him and hold out the treat as you ask "School?" He will see you approaching with a treat in your hand and most likely begin walking toward you. As you meet, give him the treat and praise again.

The third time, ask the question, have a treat in your hand and walk only a short distance toward the dog so that he must walk almost all the way to you. As he reaches you, give him the treat and praise again.

By this time, the dog will probably be getting the idea that if he pays attention to you, especially when you ask that question, it will pay off in treats and enjoyable activities for him. In other words, he learns that "school" means doing great things with you

SAFETY FIRST

While it may seem that the most important things to your dog are eating, sleeping and chewing the upholstery on your furniture, his first concern is actually safety. The domesticated dogs we keep as companions have the same pack instinct as their ancestors who ran free thousands of years ago. Because of this pack instinct, your dog wants to know that he and his pack are not in danger of being harmed, and that his pack has a strong, capable leader. You must establish yourself as the leader early on in your relationship. That way your dog will trust that you will take care of him and the pack, and he will accept your commands without question.

hold it in your left hand and a food treat in your right. Place your food hand at the dog's nose and let him lick the treat but not take it from you. Say "Sit" and slowly raise your food hand from in front of the dog's nose up over his head so that he is looking at the sky. As he bends his head upward, he will have to bend his knees to maintain his balance. As he bends his knees, he will

When teaching the Akita to sit, a little pressure on the hindquarters is helpful for the stubborn student.

that are fun and result in positive attention for him.

Remember that the dog does not understand your verbal language; he only recognizes sounds. Your question translates to a series of sounds for him, and those sounds become the signal to go to you and pay attention; if he does, he will get to interact with you plus receive treats and praise.

THE BASIC COMMANDS

TEACHING SIT

Now that you have the dog's attention, attach his lead and

assume a sit position. At that point, release the food treat and praise lavishly with comments such as "Good dog! Good sit!" Remember to always praise enthusiastically, because dogs relish verbal praise from their owners and feel so proud of themselves whenever they accomplish a behavior.

You will not use food forever in getting the dog to obey your commands. Food is only used to teach new behaviors, and once the dog knows what you want when you give a specific command, you will wean him off the food treats but still maintain the verbal praise. After all, you will always have your voice with you, and there will be many times when you have no food rewards but expect the dog to obey.

Always practice obedience commands on lead until the Akita is reliably trained.

LANGUAGE BARRIER

Dogs do not understand our language and have to rely on tone of voice more than just words or sound. They can be trained to react to a certain sound, at a certain volume. If you say "No, Ko-Go" in a very soft, pleasant voice, it will not have the same meaning as "No, Ko-Go!!" when you raise your voice.

You should never use the dog's name during a reprimand, just the command "No! " You never want the dog to associate his name with a negative experience or reprimand.

TEACHING DOWN

Teaching the down exercise is easy when you understand how the dog perceives the down position, and it is very difficult when you do not. Dogs perceive the down position as a submissive one, therefore teaching the down exercise using a forceful method can sometimes make the dog develop such a fear of the down that he either runs away when you say "Down" or he attempts to snap at the person who tries to force him down. Thus is particularly so with a dog as naturally dominant as the Akita.

Have the dog sit closealongside your left leg, facing in the same direction as you are. Hold the lead in your left hand and a food treat in your right. Now

help calm the dog as he tries to follow the food hand in order to get the treat.

When the dog's elbows touch the floor, release the food and praise softly. Try to get the dog to maintain that down position for several seconds before you let him sit up again. The goal here is to get the dog to settle down and not feel threatened in the down position.

TEACHING STAY

It is easy to teach the dog to stay in either a sit or a down position.

The down-stay is an extension of the down command. Use hand signals and voice commands to execute this exercise.

place your left hand lightly on the top of the dog's shoulders where they meet above the spinal cord. Do not push down on the dog's shoulders; simply rest your left hand there so you can guide the dog to lie down close to your left leg rather than to swing away from your side when he drops.

Now place the food hand at the dog's nose, say "Down" very softly (almost a whisper), and slowly lower the food hand to the dog's front feet. When the food hand reaches the floor, begin moving it forward along the floor in front of the dog. Keep talking softly to the dog, saying things like, "Do you want this treat? You can do this, good dog." Your reassuring tone of voice will

DOUBLE JEOPARDY

A dog in jeopardy never lies down. He stays alert on his feet because instinct tells him that he may have to run away or fight for his survival. Therefore, if a dog feels threatened or anxious, he will not lie down. Consequently, it is important to keep the dog calm and relaxed as he learns the down exercise.

CONSISTENCY PAYS OFF

Dogs need consistency in their feeding schedule, exercise and relief visits, and in the verbal commands you use. If you use "Stay" on Monday and "Stay here, please" on Tuesday, you will confuse your dog. Don't demand perfect behavior during training sessions and then let him have the run of the house the rest of the day. Above all, lavish praise on your pet consistently every time he does something right. The more he feels he is pleasing you, the more willing he will be to learn.

Again, we use food and praise during the teaching process as we help the dog to understand exactly what it is that we are expecting him to do.

To teach the sit/stay, start with the dog sitting on your left side as before and hold the lead in your left hand. Have a food treat in your right hand and place your food hand at the dog's nose. Say "Stay" and step out on your right foot to stand directly in front of the dog, toe to toe, as he licks and nibbles the treat. Be sure to keep his head facing upward to maintain the sit position. Count to five and then swing around to stand next to the dog again with him on your left. As soon as you get back to the original position, release the food and praise lavishly.

To teach the down/stay, do the down as previously described. As soon as the dog lies down, say "Stay" and step out on your right foot just as you did in the sit/stay. Count to five and then return to stand beside the dog with him on your left side. Release the treat and praise as always.

Within a week or ten days, you can begin to add a bit of distance between you and your dog when you leave him. When you do, use your left hand open with the palm facing the dog as a stay signal, much the same as the hand signal a traffic cop uses to stop traffic at an intersection. Hold the food treat in your right hand as before, but this time the food is not touching the dog's nose. He will watch the food hand and quickly learn that he is going to get that treat as soon as you return to his side.

When you can stand 3 feet away from your dog for 30 seconds, you can then begin building time and distance in both stays. Eventually, the dog can be expected to remain in the stay position for prolonged periods of time until you return to him or call him to you. Always praise lavishly when he stays.

TEACHING COME

If you make teaching "come" an exciting experience, you should never have a student that does not love the game or that fails to come when called. The secret, it seems, is never to teach the word "come."

At times when an owner most wants his dog to come when called, the owner is likely to be upset or anxious and he allows these feelings to come through in the tone of his voice when he calls his dog. Hearing that desperation in his owner's voice, the dog fears the results of going to him and therefore either disobeys outright or runs in the opposite direction. The secret, therefore, is to teach the dog a game and, when you want him to come to you, simply play the game. It is practically a no-fail solution!

To begin, have several members of your family take a few food treats and each go into a different room in the house. Take turns calling the dog, and each person should celebrate the dog's finding him with a treat and lots of happy praise. When a person calls the dog, he is actually invit-

"WHERE ARE YOU?"
When calling the dog, do not say "Come." Say things like, "Sumi, where are you? See if you can find me! I have a biscuit for you!" Keep up a constant line of chatter with coaxing sounds and frequent questions such as, "Where are you?" The dog will learn to follow the sound of your voice to locate you and receive his reward.

"COME" ... BACK

Never call your dog to come to you for a correction or scold him when he reaches you. That is the quickest way to turn a come command into "Go away fast!" Dogs think only in the present tense, and your dog will connect the scolding with coming to you, not with the misbehavior of a few moments earlier.

ing the dog to find him and get a treat as a reward for "winning."

A few turns of the "Where are you?" game and the dog will understand that everyone is playing the game and that each person has a big celebration awaiting his success at locating them. Once he learns to love the game, simply calling out "Where are you?" will bring him running from wherever he is when he hears that all-important question.

The come command is recognized as one of the most important things to teach a dog, but there are trainers who work with thousands of dogs and never teach the actual word "come." Yet these dogs will race to respond to a person who uses the dog's name followed by "Where are you?" For example, a woman has a 12-year-old companion dog who went blind, but who never fails to locate her owner when asked, "Where are you?"

Children, in particular, love to play this game with their dogs. Children can hide in smaller places like a shower stall or bathtub, behind a bed or under a table. The dog needs to work a little bit harder to find these hiding places, but when he does he loves to celebrate with a treat and a tussle with a favorite youngster.

TEACHING HEEL

Heeling means that the dog walks beside the owner without pulling. It takes time and patience on the owner's part to succeed at teaching the dog that he (the owner) will not proceed unless the dog is walking calmly beside him. Pulling out ahead on the lead is definitely not acceptable.

Begin by holding the lead in your left hand as the dog sits beside your left leg. Move the loop end of the lead to your right hand but keep your left hand short on the lead so it keeps the dog in close next to you.

Say "Heel" and step forward on your left foot. Keep the dog close to you and take three steps. Stop and have the dog sit next to you in what we now call the heel position. Praise verbally, but do not touch the dog. Hesitate a moment and begin again with "Heel," taking three steps and stopping, at which point the dog is told to sit again.

Your goal here is to have the dog walk those three steps without pulling on the lead. Once he will walk calmly beside you for three steps without pulling, increase the number of steps you take to five. When he will walk politely beside you while you take five steps, you can increase the length of your walk to ten steps. Keep increasing the length of your stroll until the dog will walk quietly beside you without pulling as long as you want him to heel. When you stop heeling, indicate to the dog that the exercise is over by verbally praising as you pet him and say "OK, good dog." The "OK" is used as a release word, meaning that the exercise is finished and the dog is free to relax.

If you are dealing with a dog who insists on pulling you around, simply "put on your brakes" and stand your ground until the dog realizes that the two of you are not going anywhere until he is beside you and moving at your pace, not his. It may take some time just standing there to convince the dog that you are the leader and you will be the one to decide on the direction and speed of your travel.

HEELING WELL

Teach your dog to heel in an enclosed area. Once you think the dog will obey reliably and you want to attempt advanced obedience exercises such as off-lead heeling, test him in a fenced-in area so he cannot run away.

HOW TO WEAN THE "TREAT HOG"

If you have trained your dog by rewarding him with a treat each time he performs a command, he may soon decide that without the treat, he won't sit, stay or come. The best way to fix this problem is to start asking your dog to do certain commands twice before being rewarded. Slowly increase the number of commands given and then vary the number: three sits and a treat one day, five sits for a biscuit the next day, etc. Your dog will soon realize that there is no set number of sits before he gets his reward and he'll likely do it the first time you ask in the hope of being rewarded sooner rather than later.

Each time the dog looks up at you or slows down to give a slack lead between the two of you, quietly praise him and say, "Good heel. Good dog." Eventually, the dog will begin to respond and within a few days he will be walking politely beside you without pulling on the lead. At first, the training sessions should be kept short and very positive; soon the dog will be able to walk nicely with you for increasingly longer distances. Remember also to give the dog free time and the opportunity to run and play when you have finished heel practice.

WEANING OFF FOOD IN TRAINING

Food is used in training new behaviors. Once the dog understands what behavior goes with a specific command, it is time to start weaning him off the food treats. At first, give a treat after each exercise. Then, start to give a treat only after every other exercise. Mix up the times when you offer a food reward and the times when you offer only praise so that the dog will never know when he is going to receive both food and praise and when he is going to receive only praise. This is called a variable-ratio-reward system and it proves successful because there is always the chance that the owner will produce a treat, so the dog never stops trying for that reward. No matter what, *always* give verbal praise.

OBEDIENCE CLASSES

It is a good idea to enroll in an obedience class if one is available in your area. If yours is a show dog, conformation training classes would be more appropriate. Many areas have dog clubs that offer basic obedience training as well as preparatory classes for obedience competition. There are also local dog trainers who offer similar classes.

At obedience trials, dogs can earn titles at various levels of competition. The beginning levels of competition include basic behaviors such as sit, down, heel, etc. The more advanced levels of competition

OBEDIENCE SCHOOL
A basic obedience beginner's class usually lasts for six to eight weeks. Dog and owner attend an hour-long lesson once a week and practice for a few minutes, several times a day, each day at home. If done properly, the whole procedure will result in a well-mannered dog and an owner who delights in living with a pet that is eager to please and enjoys doing things with his owner.

include jumping, retrieving, scent discrimination and signal work. The advanced levels require a dog and owner to put a lot of time and effort into their training and the titles that can be earned at these levels of competition are very prestigious.

With patience and consistent training, the Akita can learn anything. This Akita is learning to tango.

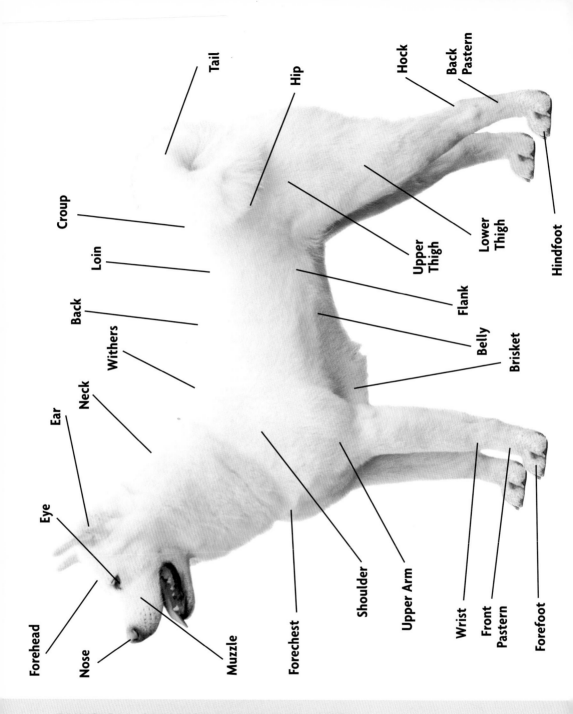

Tail

Hip

Hock

Back Pastern

Croup

Loin

Upper Thigh

Lower Thigh

Hindfoot

Back

Flank

Withers

Belly

Neck

Brisket

Ear

Eye

Forehead

Nose

Muzzle

Forechest

Shoulder

Upper Arm

Wrist

Front Pastern

Forefoot

PHYSICAL STRUCTURE OF THE AKITA

AKITA

Dogs suffer from many of the same physical illnesses as people. They might even share many of the same psychological problems. Since people usually know more about human diseases than canine maladies, many of the terms used in this chapter will be familiar but not necessarily those used by veterinarians. We will use the term *x-ray*, instead of the more acceptable term *radiograph*. We will also use the familiar term *symptoms* even though dogs don't have symptoms, which are verbal descriptions of the patient's feelings; dogs have *clinical signs*. Since dogs can't speak, we have to look for clinical signs...but we still use the term *symptoms* in this book.

As a general rule, medicine is *practiced*. That term is not arbitrary. Medicine is a constantly changing art as we learn more and more about genetics, electronic aids (like CAT scans and MRIs) and daily laboratory advances. There are many dog maladies, like canine hip dysplasia, which are not universally treated in the same manner. Some veterinarians opt for surgery more often than others do.

SELECTING A VETERINARIAN

Your selection of a veterinarian should be based not only upon personality and ability with large-bred dogs but also upon his convenience to your home. You want a vet who is close because you might have emergencies or need to make multiple visits for treatments. You want a vet who has services that you might require such as tattooing and grooming, as well as sophisticated pet supplies and a good reputation for ability and responsiveness. There is nothing more frustrating than having to wait a day or more to get a response from your veterinarian.

All veterinarians are licensed and their diplomas and/or certifi-

NEUTERING/SPAYING
Male dogs are castrated. The operation removes both testicles and requires that the dog be anesthetized. Recovery takes about one week. Females are spayed; in this operation, the uterus (womb) and both of the ovaries are removed. This is major surgery, also carried out under general anesthesia, and it usually takes a bitch two weeks to recover.

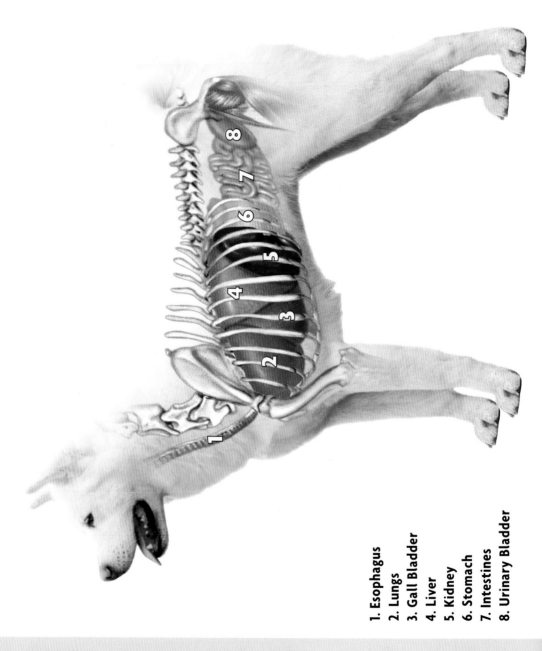

1. Esophagus
2. Lungs
3. Gall Bladder
4. Liver
5. Kidney
6. Stomach
7. Intestines
8. Urinary Bladder

INTERNAL ORGANS OF THE AKITA

cates should be displayed in their waiting rooms. There are, however, many veterinary specialties that usually require further studies and internships. There are specialists in heart problems (veterinary cardiologists), skin problems (veterinary dermatologists), teeth and gum problems (veterinary dentists), eye problems (veterinary ophthalmologists) and x-rays (veterinary radiologists), as well as vets who have specialties in bones, muscles or certain organs. Most veterinarians do routine surgery such as neutering, stitching up wounds and docking tails for those breeds in which such is required for show purposes. When the problem affecting your dog is serious, it is not unusual or impudent to get another medical opinion, although it is courteous to advise the vets concerned about this. You might also want to compare costs among several veterinarians. Sophisticated health care and veterinary services can be very costly. Sometimes important decisions must be based upon financial considerations.

PREVENTATIVE MEDICINE

It is much easier, less costly and more effective to practice preventative medicine than to fight bouts of illness and disease. Properly bred puppies come from parents who were selected based upon their genetic-disease profiles.

Breakdown of Veterinary Income by Category

2%	Dentistry
4%	Radiology
12%	Surgery
15%	Vaccinations
19%	Laboratory
23%	Examinations
25%	Medicines

Their dam should have been vaccinated, free of all internal and external parasites and properly nourished. For these reasons, a visit to the veterinarian who cared for the dam is recommended. The dam can pass on disease resistance to her puppies, which can last for eight to ten weeks. She can also pass on parasites and many infections. That's why you should learn as much about the health of the dam as possible.

VACCINATION SCHEDULING

Most vaccinations are given by injection and should only be done by a veterinarian. Both he and you should keep a record of the date of the injection, the identification of the vaccine and the amount given. Some vets give a first vaccination at eight weeks, but most dog breeders prefer the course not to commence until about ten weeks because of negating any antibodies passed on by the dam.

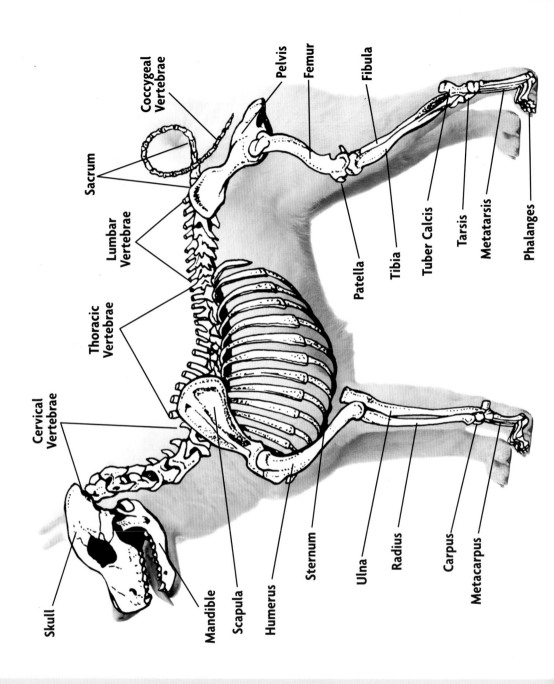

Coccygeal
Vertebrae

Pelvis

Femur

Fibula

Sacrum

Lumbar
Vertebrae

Patella

Tibia

Tuber Calcis

Tarsis

Metatarsis

Phalanges

Thoracic
Vertebrae

Cervical
Vertebrae

Skull

Mandible

Scapula

Humerus

Sternum

Ulna

Radius

Carpus

Metacarpus

SKELETAL STRUCTURE OF THE AKITA

The vaccination scheduling is usually based on a 15-day cycle. You must take your vet's advice regarding when to vaccinate as this may differ according to the vaccine used. Most vaccinations immunize your puppy against viruses.

The usual vaccines contain immunizing doses of several different viruses such as distemper, parvovirus, parainfluenza and hepatitis although some veterinarians recommend separate vaccines for each disease. There are other vaccines available when the puppy is at risk. You should rely

KNOW WHEN TO POSTPONE A VACCINATION

While the visit to the vet is costly, it is never advisable to update a vaccination when visiting with a sick or pregnant dog. Vaccinations should be avoided for all elderly dogs. If your dog is showing the signs of any illness or any medical condition, no matter how serious or mild, including skin irritations, do not vaccinate. Likewise, a lame dog should never be vaccinated; any dog undergoing surgery or on any immunosuppressant drugs should not be vaccinated until fully recovered.

HEALTH AND VACCINATION SCHEDULE

AGE IN WEEKS:	6TH	8TH	10TH	12TH	14TH	16TH	20-24TH	52ND
Worm Control	✔	✔	✔	✔	✔	✔	✔	
Neutering							✔	
Heartworm		✔		✔		✔	✔	
Parvovirus	✔		✔		✔		✔	✔
Distemper		✔		✔		✔		✔
Hepatitis		✔		✔		✔		✔
Leptospirosis								✔
Parainfluenza	✔		✔		✔			✔
Dental Examination		✔					✔	✔
Complete Physical		✔					✔	✔
Coronavirus				✔			✔	✔
Canine Cough	✔							
Hip Dysplasia								✔
Rabies							✔	

Vaccinations are not instantly effective. It takes about two weeks for the dog's immune system to develop antibodies. Most vaccinations require annual booster shots. Your vet should guide you in this regard.

Normal hairs of a dog enlarged 200 times original size. The cuticle (outer covering) is clean and healthy. Unlike human hair that grows from the base, a dog's hair also grows from the end, as shown in the inset.

S.E.M. BY DR. DENNIS KUNKEL, UNIVERSITY OF HAWAII

upon professional advice. This is especially true for the booster-shot program. Most vaccination programs require a booster when the puppy is a year old and once a year thereafter. In some cases, circumstances may require more or less frequent immunizations. Canine cough, more formally known as tracheobronchitis, is treated with a vaccine that is sprayed into the dog's nostrils. Canine cough is usually included in routine vaccination, but this is often not so effective as for other major diseases.

WEANING TO FIVE MONTHS OLD

Puppies should be weaned by the time they are about two months old. A puppy that remains for at least eight weeks with its mother and littermates usually adapts better to other dogs and people later in its life.

Some new owners have their puppy examined by a veterinarian immediately, which is a good idea. Vaccination programs usually begin when the puppy is very young.

The puppy will have his teeth examined and have his skeletal conformation and general health checked prior to certification by the veterinarian. Puppies in certain breeds have problems with their kneecaps, cataracts and other eye problems, heart murmurs and undescended testicles. They may also have personality problems and your veterinarian might have training in temperament evaluation.

FIVE TO TWELVE MONTHS OF AGE

Unless you intend to breed or show your dog, neutering the puppy at six months of age is recommended. Discuss this with your veterinarian. Neutering has proven to be extremely beneficial to both male and female puppies. Besides eliminating the possibility of pregnancy and pyometra in bitches and testicular cancer in male dogs, it inhibits (but does not prevent) breast cancer in bitches and prostate cancer in dogs. Under no circumstances should a bitch be spayed prior to her first season.

Your veterinarian should provide your puppy with a thorough dental evaluation at six months of age, ascertaining whether all of the permanent teeth have erupted properly. A home dental-care regimen should

PUPPY VACCINATIONS

Your veterinarian will probably recommend that your puppy be fully vaccinated before you take him outside. There are airborne diseases, parasite eggs in the grass and unexpected visits from other dogs that might be dangerous to your puppy's health. Other dogs are the most harmful reservoir of pathogenic organisms, as everything they have can be transmitted to your puppy.

DISEASE REFERENCE CHART

	What is it?	What causes it?	Symptoms
Leptospirosis	Severe disease that affects the internal organs; can be spread to people.	A bacterium, which is often carried by rodents, that enters through mucous membranes and spreads quickly throughout the body.	Range from fever, vomiting and loss of appetite in less severe cases to shock, irreversible kidney damage and possibly death in most severe cases.
Rabies	Potentially deadly virus that infects warm-blooded mammals.	Bite from a carrier of the virus, mainly wild animals.	1st stage: dog exhibits change in behavior, fear. 2nd stage: dog's behavior becomes more aggressive. 3rd stage: loss of coordination, trouble with bodily functions.
Parvovirus	Highly contagious virus, potentially deadly.	Ingestion of the virus, which is usually spread through the feces of infected dogs.	Most common: severe diarrhea. Also vomiting, fatigue, lack of appetite.
Canine cough	Contagious respiratory infection.	Combination of types of bacteria and virus. Most common: *Bordetella bronchiseptica* bacteria and parainfluenza virus.	Chronic cough.
Distemper	Disease primarily affecting respiratory and nervous system.	Virus that is related to the human measles virus.	Mild symptoms such as fever, lack of appetite and mucus secretion progress to evidence of brain damage, "hard pad."
Hepatitis	Virus primarily affecting the liver.	Canine adenovirus type I (CAV-1). Enters system when dog breathes in particles.	Lesser symptoms include listlessness, diarrhea, vomiting. More severe symptoms include "blue-eye" (clumps of virus in eye).
Coronavirus	Virus resulting in digestive problems.	Virus is spread through infected dog's feces.	Stomach upset evidenced by lack of appetite, vomiting, diarrhea.

be initiated at six months, including brushing weekly and providing good dental devices (such as nylon bones). Regular dental care promotes healthy teeth, fresh breath and a longer life.

OVER ONE YEAR OF AGE

Once a year, your full-grown dog should visit the vet for an examination and vaccination boosters, if needed. Some vets recommend blood tests, thyroid level check and dental evaluation to accompany these annual visits. A thorough clinical evaluation by the vet can provide critical background information for your dog. Blood tests are often performed at

VITAL SIGNS

A dog's normal temperature is 101.5 degrees Fahrenheit. A range of between 100.0 and 102.5 degrees should be considered normal, as each dog's body sets its own temperature. It will be helpful if you take your dog's temperature when you know he is healthy and record it. Then, when you suspect that he is not feeling well, you will have a normal figure to compare the abnormal temperature against.

The normal pulse rate for a dog is between 100 and 125 beats per minute.

one year of age, and dental examinations around the third or fourth birthday. In the long run, quality preventative care for your pet can save money, teeth and lives.

HEREDITARY PROBLEMS IN AKITAS

HYPOTHYROIDISM

Defined as the lessening of thyroid hormone production, hypothyroidism usually results in poor coat, dry or thickened skin, lowered resistance to disease, obesity, heat-seeking, irritability and/or general malaise and lethargy. There is strong evidence that a diet free of chemicals and preservatives will greatly reduce the chance of glandular and organ disease. The thyroid gland is considered a "master" gland and, as such, is responsible for many other organs. A blood test is necessary to check blood levels of thyroid hormone and should be a part of a yearly exam. Akitas and other large-breed dogs are more prone to underactive thyroid than most other breeds.

HIP DYSPLASIA

Simply stated, hip dysplasia (HD) means the abnormal or poor development of the hip joint. It occurs most commonly in large breeds of dog and is known to be inherited. A severe case can render a working dog worthless, and even a mild case can cause

painful arthritis in the average house dog. Diagnosed only through x-ray examination, less severe cases may go undetected

DENTAL HEALTH

A dental examination is in order when the dog is between six months and one year of age so that any permanent teeth that have erupted incorrectly can be corrected. It is important to begin a brushing routine at home, using dental-care products made for dogs, such as special toothbrushes and toothpaste. Durable nylon and safe edible chews should be a part of your puppy's arsenal for good health, good teeth and pleasant breath. The vast majority of dogs three to four years old and older has diseases of the gums from lack of dental attention. Using the various types of dental chews can be very effective in controlling dental plaque.

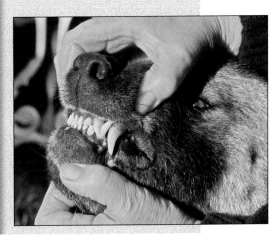

until the dog's ability to move normally becomes impaired.

While hip dysplasia is largely an inherited condition, research shows that environmental factors play a significant role in its development. Overfeeding and feeding a diet high in calories (primarily fat) during a puppy's rapid-growth stages are suspected to be contributing factors to the development of HD, and heavy-bodied and overweight puppies are more at risk than pups with very lean conformation. Breeders have found that providing the litter with non-slip flooring in the whelping pen can also ward off possible problems that can result from the puppy's injuring their ligaments. This is especially relevant with puppies as heavy as Akitas!

The Orthopedic Foundation for Animals functions as a hip and elbow registry, keeping records on all pure-bred dogs in the country that have been x-rayed for hip

MORE THAN VACCINES

Vaccinations help prevent your new puppy from contracting diseases, but they do not cure them. Proper nutrition as well as parasite control keep your dog healthy and less susceptible to many dangerous diseases. Remember that your dog depends on you to ensure his well-being.

dysplasia, elbow dypslasia and many other hereditary diseases. An Akita who is 24 months of age or older must be evaluated by three board-certified OFA radiologists who score the dog's hips as "Excellent," "Good" and "Fair." Any Akita with these passing grades is an eligible candidate for a breeding program. Akitas that score "Borderline," "Mild," "Moderate" and "Severe" are not eligible for breeding. The sire and dam of your new puppy should have OFA evaluations, proving that they were eligible for breeding. The purpose of such screening is to eliminate affected dogs from breeding programs, with the long-term goal of reducing the occurrence of HD in affected breeds.

VON WILLEBRAND'S DISEASE
Considered the most common bleeding disorder of pure-bred dogs, von Willebrand's disease (vWD) can be inherited from one or both parents. The disease can

VACCINE ALLERGIES

Vaccines do not work all the time. Sometimes dogs are allergic to them and many times the antibodies, which are supposed to be stimulated by the vaccine, just are not produced. You should keep your dog in the veterinary clinic for an hour after it is vaccinated to be sure there are no allergic reactions.

DO YOU KNOW ABOUT HIP DYSPLASIA?

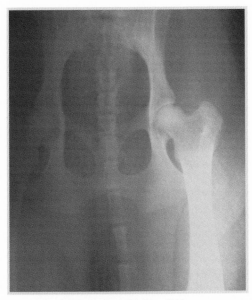

X-ray of a dog with "Good" hips.

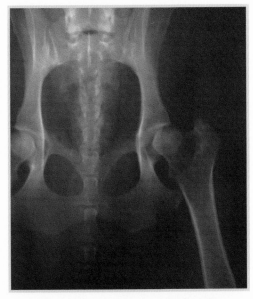

X-ray of a dog with "Moderate" dysplastic hips.

Hip dysplasia is a fairly common condition found in pure-bred dogs. When a dog has hip dysplasia, his hind leg has an incorrectly formed hip joint. By constant use of the hip joint, it becomes more and more loose, wears abnormally and may become arthritic.

Hip dysplasia can only be confirmed with an x-ray, but certain symptoms may indicate a problem. Your dog may have a hip dysplasia problem if he walks in a peculiar manner, hops instead of smoothly runs, uses his hind legs in unison (to keep the pressure off the weak joint), has trouble getting up from a prone position or always sits with both legs together on one side of his body.

As the dog matures, he may adapt well to life with a bad hip, but in a few years the arthritis develops and many dogs with hip dysplasia become crippled.

Hip dysplasia is considered an inherited disease and only can be diagnosed definitively by x-ray when the dog is two years old, although symptoms often appear earlier. Some experts claim that a special diet might help your puppy outgrow the bad hip, but the usual treatments are surgical. The removal of the pectineus muscle, the removal of the round part of the femur, reconstructing the pelvis and replacing the hip with an artificial one are all surgical interventions that are expensive, but they are usually very successful. Follow the advice of your veterinarian.

also be acquired in association with familial hypothyroidism. Bleeding disorders usually result from clotting deficiencies or platelet defects. Inquire of your veterinarian for vWD tests to determine the level of clotting factor in your dog's blood. Whether a breeding animal or a pet puppy, an average amount of clotting factor should be present in the blood. Pet owners should investigate this factor before spaying or neutering their Akitas, since a pup badly affected with vWD could bleed profusely at surgery or develop a hematoma. Discuss this with your vet and breeder.

PROGRESSIVE RETINAL ATROPHY
PRA, as progressive retinal atrophy is known, is a defect of the retina (or light receptor area of the eye). PRA can be diagnosed only by a veterinarian through ophthalmologic examination. As the name indicates, PRA is progressive and,

The Eyes Have It!

Eye disease is more prevalent among dogs than most people think, ranging from slight infections that are easily treated to serious complications that can lead to permanent sight loss. Eye diseases need veterinary attention in their early stages to prevent irreparable damage. This list provides descriptions of some common eye diseases:

Cataracts: Symptoms are white or gray discoloration of the eye lens and pupil, which causes fuzzy or completely obscured vision. Surgical treatment is required to remove the damaged lens and replace it with an artificial one.

Conjunctivitis: An inflammation of the mucus membrane that lines the eye socket, leaving the eyes red and puffy with excessive discharge. This condition is easily treated with antibiotics.

Corneal damage: The cornea is the transparent covering of the iris and pupil. Injuries are difficult to detect, but manifest themselves in surface abnormality, redness, pain and discharge. Most infections of the cornea are treated with antibiotics and require immediate medical attention.

Dry eye: This condition is caused by deficient production of tears that lubricate and protect the eye surface. A telltale sign is yellow-green discharge. Left undiagnosed, your dog will experience considerable pain, infections and possibly blindness. Dry eye is commonly treated with antibiotics, although more advanced cases may require surgery.

Glaucoma: This is caused by excessive fluid pressure in the eye. Symptoms are red eyes, gray or blue discoloration, pain, enlarged eyeballs and loss of vision. Antibiotics sometimes help, but surgery may be needed.

as the retina atrophies or degenerates, the disease leads to eventual total blindness.

Unfortunately, owners may not be aware of the condition in their dogs until it has progressed to near blindness. Akitas adapt quite well to their gradually reduced vision, making it difficult for owners to notice the changes in the dogs' behavior. Any dog affected by PRA must be removed from a breeding program.

CERF, which is the Canine Eye Registration Foundation, serves as a national registry devised to control the spread of hereditary eye diseases in pure-bred dogs. The organization works with

MANY KINDS OF EARS
Not every dog's ears are the same. Ears that are open to the air are healthier than ears with poor air circulation. Sometimes a dog can have two differently shaped ears. You should not probe inside your dog's ears. Only clean that which is accessible with a cotton ball.

board-certified veterinary ophthalmologists who are members of the American College of Veterinary Ophthalmologists (ACVO). CERF has accumulated a database of all dogs who have been examined to an ACVO Diplomate, which assists vets and breeders in eliminating diseases like PRA, inherited cataracts and retinal dysplasia from pure-bred dog breeds. The puppy that you acquire should have been bred from parents who have been screened by CERF.

A SKUNKY PROBLEM
Have you noticed your dog dragging his rump along the floor? If so, it is likely that his anal sacs are impacted or possibly infected. The anal sacs are small pouches located on both sides of the anus under the skin and muscles. They are about the size and shape of a grape and contain a foul-smelling liquid. Their contents are usually emptied when the dog has a bowel movement but, if not emptied completely, they will impact, which will cause your dog much pain. Fortunately, your veterinarian can tend to this problem easily by draining the sacs for the dog. Be aware that your dog might also empty his anal sacs in cases of extreme fright.

PARVO FOR THE COURSE

Canine parvovirus is an highly contagious disease that attacks puppies and older dogs. Spread through contact with infected feces, parvovirus causes bloody diarrhea, vomiting, heart damage, dehydration, shock and death. To prevent this tragedy, breeders have their puppies begin their series of vaccinations at six to eight weeks of age. Be aware that the virus is easily spread and is carried on a dog's hair, feet, water bowls and other objects, as well as on people's shoes and clothing.

SKIN PROBLEMS IN AKITAS

Veterinarians are consulted by dog owners for skin problems more than for any other group of diseases or maladies. Dogs' skin is almost as sensitive as human skin and both suffer from almost the same ailments (though the occurrence of acne in dogs is rare!). For this reason, veterinary dermatology has developed into a specialty practiced by many veterinarians.

Since many skin problems have visual symptoms that are almost identical, it requires the skill of an experienced veterinary

Vitamins Recommended for Dogs

Some breeders and vets recommend the supplementation of vitamins to a dog's diet—others do not. Before embarking on a vitamin program, consult your vet.

Vitamin / Dosage	Food source	Benefits
A / 10,000 IU/week	Eggs, butter, yogurt, meat	Skin, eyes, hind legs, haircoat
B / Varies	Organs, cottage cheese, sardines	Appetite, fleas, heart, skin and coat
C / 2000 mg+	Fruit, legumes, leafy green vegetables	Healing, arthritis, kidneys
D / Varies	Cod liver, cheese, organs, eggs	Bones, teeth, endocrine system
E / 250 IU daily	Leafy green vegetables, meat, wheat germ oil	Skin, muscles, nerves, healing, digestion
F / Varies	Fish oils, raw meat	Heart, skin, coat, fleas
K / Varies	Naturally in body, not through food	Blood clotting

dermatologist to identify and cure many of the more severe skin disorders. Pet shops sell many treatments for skin problems but most of the treatments are directed at symptoms and not the underlying problem(s). If your dog is suffering from a skin disorder, you should seek professional assistance as quickly as possible. As with all diseases, the earlier a problem is identified and treated, the more successful is the cure.

CONTACT DERMATITIS

Pemphigus, a condition marked by the loss of pigment in the nose, appears as contact dermatitis in Akitas. Similarly, contact dermatitis resulting from pine tar residue may affect the Akita's underbelly. This condition is a result of the dog's lying on your newly cleaned floors. Pine-based disinfectants should be avoided in homes with dogs or cats.

"P" STANDS FOR PROBLEM

Urinary tract disease is a serious condition that requires immediate medical attention. Symptoms include urinating in inappropriate places or the need to urinate frequently in small amounts. Urinary-tract disease is most effectively treated with antibiotics. To help promote good urinary-tract health, owners must always be sure that a constant supply of fresh water is available to their pets.

HEREDITARY SKIN DISORDERS

Veterinary dermatologists are currently researching a number of skin disorders that are believed to have hereditary bases. These inherited diseases are transmitted by both parents, who appear (phenotypically) normal but have a recessive gene for the disease, meaning that they carry, but are not affected by, the disease. These diseases pose serious problems to breeders because in some instances there is no method of identifying carriers. Often the secondary diseases associated with these skin conditions are even more debilitating than the disorder itself, including cancers and respiratory problems.

Among the hereditary skin disorders, for which the mode of inheritance is known, are acrodermatitis, cutaneous asthenia (Ehlers-Danlos syndrome), sebaceous adenitis, cyclic hematopoiesis, dermatomyositis, IgA deficiency, color dilution alopecia and nodular dermatofibrosis. Some of these disorders are limited to one or two breeds and others affect a large number of breeds. All inherited diseases must be diagnosed and treated by a veterinary specialist.

PARASITE BITES

Many of us are allergic to insect bites. The bites itch, erupt and may even become infected. Dogs have the same reaction to fleas, ticks

and/or mites. When an insect lands on you, you have the chance to whisk it away with your hand. Unfortunately, when your dog is bitten by a flea, tick or mite, it can only scratch it away or bite it. By the time the dog has been bitten, the parasite has done some of its damage. It may also have laid eggs to cause further problems in the near future. The itching from parasite bites is probably due to the saliva injected into the site when the parasite sucks the dog's blood.

ACRAL LICK GRANULOMA

Many large dogs have a very poorly understood syndrome called acral lick granuloma. The manifestation of the problem is the dog's tireless attack at a specific area of the body, commonly the legs or paws. The dog licks so intensively that he removes the hair and skin, leaving an ugly, large wound. Tiny protuberances, which are outgrowths of new capillaries, bead on the surface of the wound. Owners who notice their dogs' biting and chewing at

their extremities should have the vet determine the cause. If acral lick granuloma is identified, although there is no absolute cure, corticosteroids are the most common treatment.

IRRITATIONS AND ALLERGIES

Another skin problem common in Akitas is "grass rash," caused by the puppy's underbelly brushing against the dew-covered grass in the morning. Adults, whose legs grow well above the grass, rarely suffer from this irritation. While

PET ADVANTAGES

If you do not intend to show or breed your new puppy, your veterinary surgeon will probably recommend that you spay your female or neuter your male. Some people believe neutering leads to weight gain, but if you feed and exercise your dog properly, this is easily avoided. Spaying or neutering can actually have many positive outcomes, such as:
• training becomes easier, as the dog focuses less on the urge to mate and more on you!
• females are protected from unplanned pregnancy as well as ovarian and uterine cancers.
• males are guarded from testicular tumours and have a reduced risk of developing prostate cancer.
  Talk to your vet regarding the right age to spay/neuter and other aspects of the procedure.

your vet may recommend an expensive treatment for this so-called puppy rash, you are best to apply some talcum powder and keep the puppy out of the grass. If you are lucky enough to live on a farm free from pesticides and other chemical pollutants, your Akita pup may be able to roll in the morning grass and not so much as itch!

Beyond toxic chemicals in the environment, your dog may be reacting to something as natural as pollen! Humans have hay fever, rose fever and other allergies from which they suffer during the pollinating season. Many dogs suffer the same allergies. When the pollen count is high, your dog might suffer but don't expect him to sneeze and have a runny nose as a human would. Dogs react to pollen allergies the same way they react to fleas—they scratch and bite themselves.

Dogs, like humans, can be tested for allergens. Discuss the testing with your veterinary dermatologist.

Fatty Risks

Any dog of any breed can suffer from obesity. Studies show that nearly 30% of our dogs are overweight, primarily from high caloric intake and low energy expenditure. The hound and gundog breeds are the most likely affected, and females are at a greater risk of obesity than males. Pet dogs that are neutered are twice as prone to obesity as intact, whole dogs.

Regardless of breed, your dog should have a visible "waist" behind his rib cage and in front of the hind legs. There should be no fatty deposits on his hips or over his rump, and his abdomen should not be extended.

Veterinary specialists link obesity with respiratory problems, cardiac disease and liver dysfunction as well as low sperm count and abnormal estrous cycles in breeding animals. Other complications include musculoskeletal disease (including arthritis), decreased immune competence, diabetes mellitus, hypothyroidism, pancreatitis and dermatosis. Other studies have indicated that excess fat leads to heat stress, as obese dogs cannot regulate their body temperatures as well as normal-weight dogs.

Don't be discouraged if you discover that your dog has a heart problem or a complicated neurological condition requiring special attention. It is possible to tend to his special medical needs. Veterinary specialists focus on areas such as cardiology, neurology and oncology. Veterinary medical associations require rigorous training and experience before granting certification in a speciality. Consulting a specialist may offer you greater peace of mind when seeking treatment for your dog.

A male dog flea, *Ctenocephalides canis.*

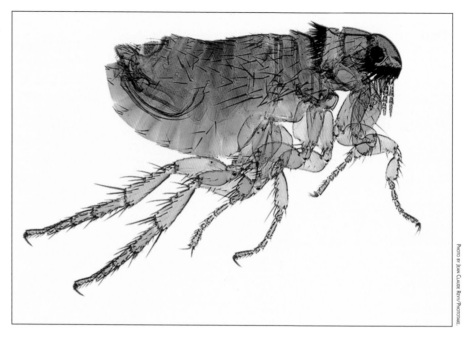

PHOTO BY JEAN CLAUDE REVY/PHOTOTAKE

EXTERNAL PARASITES

FLEAS

Of all the problems to which dogs are prone, none is more well known and frustrating than fleas. Flea infestation is relatively simple to cure but difficult to prevent. Parasites that are harbored inside the body are a bit more difficult to eradicate but they are easier to control.

To control flea infestation, you have to understand the flea's life cycle. Fleas are often thought of as a summertime problem, but centrally heated homes have changed the patterns and fleas can be found at any time of the year. The most effective method of flea control is a two-stage approach: one stage to kill the adult fleas, and the other to control the development of pre-adult fleas. Unfortunately, no single active ingredient is effective against all stages of the life cycle.

FLEA KILLER CAUTION— "POISON"

Flea-killers are poisonous. You should not spray these toxic chemicals on areas of a dog's body that he licks, including his genitals and his face. Flea killers taken internally are a better answer, but check with your vet in case internal therapy is not advised for your dog.

LIFE CYCLE STAGES

During its life, a flea will pass through four life stages: egg, larva, pupa or nymph and adult. The adult stage is the most visible and irritating stage of the flea life cycle, and this is why the majority of flea-control products concentrate on this stage. The fact is that adult fleas account for only 1% of the total flea population, and the other 99% exist in pre-adult stages, i.e., eggs, larvae and nymphs. The pre-adult stages are barely visible to the naked eye.

THE LIFE CYCLE OF THE FLEA

Eggs are laid on the dog, usually in quantities of about 20 or 30, several times a day. The adult female flea must have a blood meal before each egg-laying session. When first laid, the eggs will cling to the dog's hair, as the eggs are still moist. However, they will quickly dry out and fall from the dog, especially if the dog moves around or scratches. Many eggs will fall off in the dog's favorite area or an area in which he spends a lot of time, such as his bed.

Once the eggs fall from the dog onto the carpet or furniture, they will hatch into larvae. This takes from one to ten days. Larvae are not particularly mobile and will usually travel only a few inches from where they hatch. However, they do have a tendency to move away from bright light and heavy

**EN GARDE:
CATCHING FLEAS OFF GUARD!**
Consider the following ways to arm yourself against fleas:
- Add a small amount of pennyroyal or eucalyptus oil to your dog's bath. These natural remedies repel fleas.
- Supplement your dog's food with fresh garlic (minced or grated) and a hearty amount of brewer's yeast, both of which ward off fleas.
- Use a flea comb on your dog daily. Submerge fleas in a cup of bleach to kill them quickly.
- Confine the dog to only a few rooms to limit the spread of fleas in the home.
- Vacuum daily...and get all of the crevices! Dispose of the bag every few days until the problem is under control.
- Wash your dog's bedding daily. Cover cushions where your dog sleeps with towels, and wash the towels often.

traffic—under furniture and behind doors are common places to find high quantities of flea larvae.

The flea larvae feed on dead organic matter, including adult flea feces, until they are ready to change into adult fleas. Fleas will usually remain as larvae for around seven days. After this period, the larvae will pupate into protective pupae. While inside the pupae, the larvae will undergo

Fleas have been measured as being able to jump 300,000 times and can jump over 150 times their length in any direction, including straight up.

metamorphosis and change into adult fleas. This can take as little time as a few days, but the adult fleas can remain inside the pupae waiting to hatch for up to two years. The pupae are signaled to hatch by certain stimuli, such as physical pressure—the pupae's being stepped on, heat from an animal's lying on the pupae or increased carbon-dioxide levels and vibrations—indicating that a suitable host is available.

Once hatched, the adult flea must feed within a few days. Once the adult flea finds a host, it will not leave voluntarily. It only becomes dislodged by grooming or the host animal's scratching.

PHOTO BY DWIGHT R. KUHN.

The adult flea will remain on the host for the duration of its life unless forcibly removed.

TREATING THE ENVIRONMENT AND THE DOG

Treating fleas should be a two-pronged attack. First, the environment needs to be treated; this includes carpets and furniture, especially the dog's bedding and areas underneath furniture. The environment should be treated with a household spray containing an Insect Growth Regulator (IGR) and an insecticide to kill the adult fleas. Most IGRs are effective against eggs and larvae; they actually mimic the fleas' own hormones and stop the eggs and larvae from developing into adult fleas. There are currently no treatments available to attack the pupa stage of the life cycle, so the adult insecticide is used to kill the newly hatched adult fleas before they find a host. Most IGRs are active for many months, while

A scanning electron micrograph of a dog or cat flea, *Ctenocephalides*, magnified more than 100x. This image has been colorized for effect.

S. E. M. BY DR. DENNIS KUNKEL, UNIVERSITY OF HAWAII.

THE LIFE CYCLE OF THE FLEA

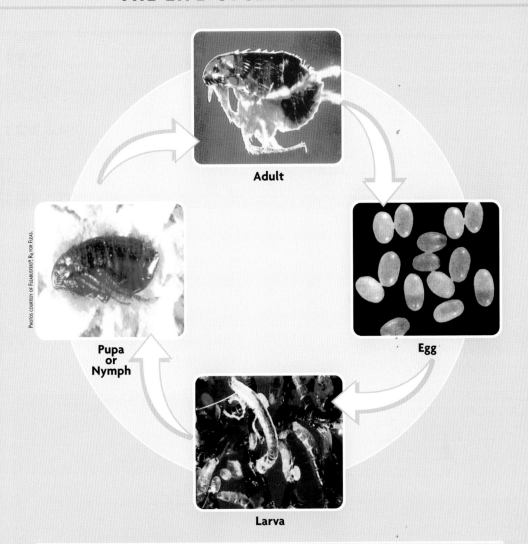

Adult

Egg

Larva

Pupa or Nymph

A LOOK AT FLEAS

Fleas have been around for millions of years and have adapted to changing host animals. They are able to go through a complete life cycle in less than one month or they can extend their lives to almost two years by remaining as pupae or cocoons. They do not need blood or any other food for up to 20 months.

INSECT GROWTH REGULATOR (IGR)

Two types of products should be used when treating fleas—a product to treat the pet and a product to treat the home. Adult fleas represent less than 1% of the flea population. The pre-adult fleas (eggs, larvae and pupae) represent more than 99% of the flea population and are found in the environment; it is in the case of pre-adult fleas that products containing an Insect Growth Regulator (IGR) should be used in the home.

IGRs are a new class of compounds used to prevent the development of insects. They do not kill the insect outright, but instead use the insect's biology against it to stop it from completing its growth. Products that contain methoprene are the world's first and leading IGRs. Used to control fleas and other insects, this type of IGR will stop flea larvae from developing and protect the house for up to seven months.

The American dog tick, *Dermacentor variabilis*, is probably the most common tick found on dogs. Look at the strength in its eight legs! No wonder it's hard to detach them.

adult insecticides are only active for a few days.

When treating with a household spray, it is a good idea to vacuum before applying the product. This stimulates as many pupae as possible to hatch into adult fleas. The vacuum cleaner should also be treated with an insecticide to prevent the eggs and larvae that have been collected in the vacuum bag from hatching.

The second stage of treatment is to apply an adult insecticide to the dog. Traditionally, this would be in the form of a collar or a spray, but more recent innovations include digestible insecticides that poison the fleas when they ingest the dog's blood. Alternatively, there are drops that, when placed on the back of the dog's neck, spread throughout the dog's hair and skin to kill adult fleas.

TICKS

Though not as common as fleas, ticks are found all over the tropical and temperate world. They don't bite, like fleas; they harpoon. They dig their sharp proboscis (nose) into the dog's skin and drink the blood. Their

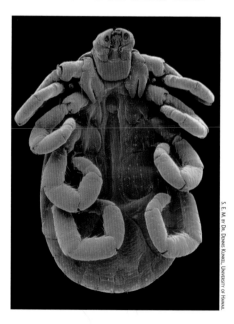

S. E. M. BY DR. DENNIS KUNKEL, UNIVERSITY OF HAWAII

only food and drink is dog's blood. Dogs can get Lyme disease, Rocky Mountain spotted fever, tick bite paralysis and many other diseases from ticks. They may live where fleas are found and they like to hide in cracks or seams in walls. They are controlled the same way fleas are controlled.

The American dog tick, *Dermacentor variabilis*, may well be the most common dog tick in many geographical areas, especially those areas where the climate is hot and humid. Most dog ticks have life expectancies of a week to six months, depending upon climatic conditions. They can neither jump nor fly, but they can crawl slowly and can range up to 16 feet to reach a sleeping or unsuspecting dog.

MITES

Just as fleas and ticks can be problematic for your dog, mites can also lead to an itchy nuisance. Microscopic in size, mites are related to ticks and generally take up permanent residence on their host animal—in this case, your dog! The term *mange* refers to any infestation caused by one of the mighty mites, of which there are six varieties that concern dog owners.

Demodex mites cause a condition known as demodicosis

DEER-TICK CROSSING

The great outdoors may be fun for your dog, but it also is home to dangerous ticks. Deer ticks carry a bacterium known as *Borrelia burgdorferi* and are most active in the autumn and spring. When infections are caught early, penicillin and tetracycline are effective antibiotics, but, if left untreated, the bacteria may cause neurological, kidney and cardiac problems as well as long-term trouble with walking and painful joints.

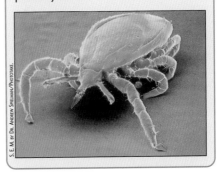

S. E. M. BY DR. ANDREW SPIELMAN/PHOTOTAKE.

PHOTO BY DR. DENNIS KUNKEL, UNIVERSITY OF HAWAII.

The head of an American dog tick, *Dermacentor variabilis*, enlarged and colorized for effect.

The mange mite, *Psoroptes bovis*, can infest cattle and other domestic animals.

PHOTO BY JAMES HANSON/YOAV/PHOTOTAKE

(sometimes called red mange or follicular mange), in which the mites live in the dog's hair follicles and sebaceous glands in larger-than-normal amounts. This type of mange is commonly passed from the dam to her puppies and usually shows up on the puppies' muzzles, though demodicosis is not transferable from one normal dog to another. Most dogs recover from this type of mange without any treatment, though topical therapies are commonly prescribed by the vet.

The *Cheyletiellosis* mite is the hook-mouthed culprit associated

Human lice look like dog lice; the two are closely related.

PHOTO BY DWIGHT R. KUHN.

with "walking dandruff," a condition that affects dogs as well as cats and rabbits. This mite lives on the surface of the animal's skin and is readily transferable through direct or indirect contact with an affected animal. The dandruff is present in the form of scaly skin, which may or may not be itchy. If not treated, this mange can affect a whole kennel of dogs and can be spread to humans as well.

The *Sarcoptes* mite causes intense itching on the dog in the form of a condition known as scabies or sarcoptic mange. The cycle of the *Sarcoptes* mite lasts about three weeks, and the mites live in the top layer of the dog's skin (epidermis), preferably in areas with little hair. Scabies is highly contagious and can be passed to humans. Sometimes an allergic reaction to the mite worsens the severe itching associated with sarcoptic mange.

Ear mites, *Otodectes cynotis,* lead to otodectic mange, which most commonly affects the outer ear canal of the dog, though other areas can be affected as well. Dogs with ear-mite infestation commonly scratch at their ears, causing further irritation, and shake their heads. Dark brown droppings in the outer ear confirm the diagnosis. Your vet can prescribe a treatment to flush out the ears and kill any eggs in the ears. A complete month of treatment is necessary to cure the mange.

Two other mites, less common in dogs, include *Dermanyssus gallinae* (the poultry or red mite) and *Eutrombicula alfreddugesi* (the North American mite associated with trombiculidiasis or chigger infestation). The poultry mite frequently lives on chickens, but can transfer to dogs who spend time near farm animals. Chigger infestation affects dogs in the

> **NOT A DROP TO DRINK**
> Never allow your dog to swim in polluted water or public areas where water quality can be suspect. Even perfectly clear water can harbor parasites, many of which can cause serious to fatal illnesses in canines. Areas inhabited by waterfowl and other wildlife are especially dangerous.

central US who have exposure to woodlands. The types of mange caused by both of these mites are treatable by veterinarians.

INTERNAL PARASITES

Most animals—fishes, birds and mammals, including dogs and humans—have worms and other parasites that live inside their bodies. According to Dr. Herbert R. Axelrod, the fish pathologist, there are two kinds of parasites: dumb and smart. The smart parasites live in peaceful cooperation with their hosts (symbiosis), while the dumb parasites kill their hosts. Most worm infections are relatively easy to control. If they are not controlled, they weaken the host dog to the point that other medical problems occur, but they do not kill the host as dumb parasites would.

> **DO NOT MIX**
> Never mix parasite-control products without first consulting your vet. Some products can become toxic when combined with others and can cause fatal consequences.

A brown dog tick, *Rhipicephalus sanguineus*, is an uncommon but annoying tick found on dogs.

PHOTO BY CAROLINA BIOLOGICAL SUPPLY/PHOTOTAKE.

The roundworm *Rhabditis* can infect both dogs and humans.

ROUNDWORMS

Average-size dogs can pass 1,360,000 roundworm eggs every day. For example, if there were only 1 million dogs in the world, the world would be saturated with thousands of tons of dog feces. These feces would contain around 15,000,000,000 roundworm eggs.

Up to 31% of home yards and children's sand boxes in the US contain roundworm eggs.

Flushing dog's feces down the toilet is not a safe practice because the usual sewage treatments do not destroy roundworm eggs.

Infected puppies start shedding roundworm eggs at three weeks of age. They can be infected by their mother's milk.

The roundworm, *Ascaris lumbricoides.*

ROUNDWORMS

The roundworms that infect dogs are known scientifically as *Toxocara canis.* They live in the dog's intestines and shed eggs continually. It has been estimated that a dog produces about 6 or more ounces of feces every day. Each ounce of feces averages hundreds of thousands of roundworm eggs. There are no known areas in which dogs roam that do not contain roundworm eggs. The greatest danger of roundworms is that they infect people, too! It is wise to have your dog tested regularly for roundworms.

In young puppies, roundworms cause bloated bellies, diarrhea, coughing and vomiting, and are transmitted from the dam (through blood or milk). Affected puppies will not appear as animated as normal puppies. The worms appear spaghetti-like, measuring as long as 6 inches. Adult dogs can acquire roundworms through coprophagia (eating contaminated feces) or by killing rodents that carry roundworms.

Roundworm infection can kill puppies and cause severe problems in adults, as the hatched larvae travel to the lungs and trachea through the bloodstream. Cleanliness is the best preventative for roundworms. Always pick up after your dog and dispose of feces in appropriate receptacles.

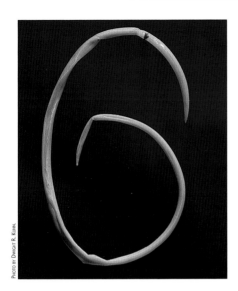

Photo by Dwight R. Kuhn.

HOOKWORMS

In the United States, dog owners have to be concerned about four different species of hookworm, the most common and most serious of which is *Ancylostoma caninum,* which prefers warm climates. The others are *Ancylostoma braziliense, Ancylostoma tubaeforme* and *Uncinaria stenocephala,* the latter of which is a concern to dogs living in the northern US and Canada, as this species prefers cold climates. Hookworms are dangerous to humans as well as to dogs and cats, and can be the cause of severe anemia due to iron deficiency. The worm uses its teeth to attach itself to the dog's intestines and changes the site of its attachment about six times per day. Each time the worm repositions itself, the dog loses

blood and can become anemic. *Ancylostoma caninum* is the most likely of the four species to cause anemia in the dog.

Symptoms of hookworm infection include dark stools, weight loss, general weakness, pale coloration and anemia, as well as possible skin problems. Fortunately, hookworms are easily purged from the affected dog with a number of medications that have proven effective. Discuss these with your veterinarian. Most heartworm preventatives include a hookworm insecticide as well.

Owners also must be aware that hookworms can infect humans, who can acquire the larvae through exposure to contaminated feces. Since the worms cannot complete their life cycle on a human, the worms simply infest the skin and cause irritation. This condition is known as cutaneous larva migrans syndrome. As a preventative, use disposable gloves or a "poop-scoop" to pick up your dog's droppings and prevent your dog (or neighborhood cats) from defecating in children's play areas.

The hookworm, *Ancylostoma caninum.*

Photo by C. James Webb/Phototake.

The infective stage of the hookworm larva.

TAPEWORMS

Humans, rats, squirrels, foxes, coyotes, wolves and domestic dogs are all susceptible to tapeworm infection. Except in humans, tapeworms are usually not a fatal infection. Infected individuals can harbor 1000 parasitic worms.

Tapeworms, like some other types of worm, are hermaphroditic, meaning male and female in the same worm.

If dogs eat infected rats or mice, or anything else infected with tapeworm, they get the tapeworm disease. One month after attaching to a dog's intestine, the worm starts shedding eggs. These eggs are infective immediately. Infective eggs can live for a few months without a host animal.

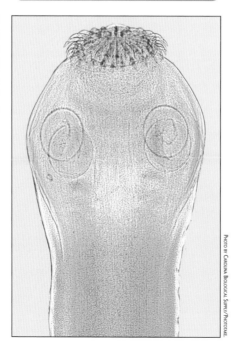

The head and rostellum (the round prominence on the scolex) of a tapeworm, which infects dogs and humans.

PHOTO BY CAROLINA BIOLOGICAL SUPPLY/PHOTOTAKE

TAPEWORMS

There are many species of tapeworm, all of which are carried by fleas! The most common tapeworm affecting dogs is known as *Dipylidium caninum*. The dog eats the flea and starts the tapeworm cycle. Humans can also be infected with tapeworms—so don't eat fleas! Fleas are so small that your dog could pass them onto your hands, your plate or your food and thus make it possible for you to ingest a flea that is carrying tapeworm eggs.

While tapeworm infection is not life-threatening in dogs (smart parasite!), it can be the cause of a very serious liver disease for humans. About 50% of the humans infected with *Echinococcus multilocularis*, a type of tapeworm that causes alveolar hydatid, perish.

WHIPWORMS

In North America, whipworms are counted among the most common parasitic worms in dogs. The whipworm's scientific name is *Trichuris vulpis*. These worms attach themselves in the lower parts of the intestine, where they feed. Affected dogs may only experience upset tummies, colic and diarrhea. These worms, however, can live for months or years in the dog, beginning their larval stage in the small intestine, spending their adult stage in the large intestine and finally passing infective eggs through the dog's feces. The only way to detect whipworms is through a fecal examination, though this is not always foolproof. Treatment for whipworms is tricky, due to the worms' unusual life-cycle pattern, and very often dogs are reinfected due to exposure to infective eggs on the ground. The whipworm eggs can survive in the environment for as long as five years; thus, cleaning up droppings in your own backyard as well as in public places is absolutely essential for sanitation purposes and the health of your dog and others.

THREADWORMS

Though less common than round-worms, hookworms and those previously mentioned, threadworms concern dog owners in the south-western US and Gulf Coast area, where the climate is hot and humid. Living in the small intestine of the dog, this worm measures a mere 2 millimeters and is round in shape. Like that of the whipworm, the threadworm's life cycle is very complex and the eggs and larvae are passed through the feces. A deadly disease in humans, *Strongyloides* readily infects people, and the handling of feces is the most common means of trans-mission. Threadworms are most often seen in young puppies; bloody diarrhea and pneumonia are symptoms. Sick puppies must be isolated and treated immediately; vets recommend a follow-up treat-ment one month later.

HEARTWORM PREVENTATIVES

There are many heartworm preventatives on the market, many of which are sold at your veterinarian's office. These products can be given daily or monthly, depending on the manufacturer's instructions. All of these preventatives contain chemical insecticides directed at killing heartworms, which leads to some controversy among dog owners. In effect, heartworm preventatives are neces-sary evils, though you should determine how necessary based on your pet's lifestyle. There is no doubt that heartworm is a dreadful disease that threatens the lives of dogs. However, the likelihood of your dog's being bitten by an infected mosquito is slim in most places, and a mosquito-repellent (or an herbal remedy such as Wormwood or Black Walnut) is much safer for your dog and will not compromise his immune system (the way heartworm preventatives will). Should you decide to use the tradi-tional preventative "medications," you can consider giving the pill every other or third month. Since the toxins in the pill will kill the heartworms at all stages of develop-ment, the pill would be effective in killing larvae, nymphs or adults and it takes four months for the larvae to reach the adult stage. Thus, there is no rationale to poison-ing the dog's system on a monthly basis. Lastly, do not give the pill during the winter months since there are no mosquitoes around to pass on their infection, unless you live in a tropical environment.

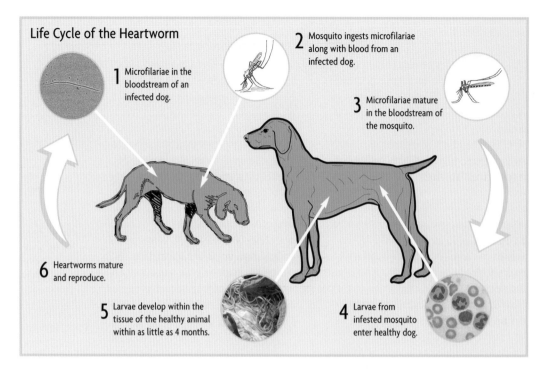

Life Cycle of the Heartworm

1 Microfilariae in the bloodstream of an infected dog.

2 Mosquito ingests microfilariae along with blood from an infected dog.

3 Microfilariae mature in the bloodstream of the mosquito.

4 Larvae from infested mosquito enter healthy dog.

5 Larvae develop within the tissue of the healthy animal within as little as 4 months.

6 Heartworms mature and reproduce.

HEARTWORMS

Heartworms are thin, extended worms up to 12 inches long, which live in a dog's heart and the major blood vessels surrounding it. Dogs may have up to 200 worms. Symptoms may be loss of energy, loss of appetite, coughing, the development of a pot belly and anemia.

Heartworms are transmitted by mosquitoes. The mosquito drinks the blood of an infected dog and takes in larvae with the blood. The larvae, called microfilariae, develop within the body of the mosquito and are passed on to the next dog bitten after the larvae mature. It takes two to three weeks for the larvae to develop to the infective stage within the body of the mosquito. Dogs are usually treated at about six weeks of age and maintained on a prophylactic dose given monthly.

Blood testing for heartworms is not necessarily indicative of how seriously your dog is infected. Although this is a dangerous disease, it is not easy for a dog to be infected. Discuss the various preventatives with your vet, as there are many different types now available. Together you can decide on a safe course of prevention for your dog.

Sadly, just like we human owners do, after so many years our pets have to grow old. The Akita is no exception. In the male Akita, for example, his mind remains active as he progresses in years, still trying to compete with the males in his area. It is a sad day indeed when he chooses to ignore the rowdy male down the lane. When he accepts that he is no longer the powerful male animal fit to take on any challenge, you are forced to realize that he is nearing the end of his time.

The Akita is considered a senior when he is seven years of age or older. For such a large breed, Akitas are, thankfully, remarkably long-lived. Sadly, a seven-year-old Great Dane is very, very old, whereas an Akita of seven years is not even ready for retirement benefits!

As he grows older, his needs will change considerably. Make sure he has a comfortable sleeping place. You might experiment with a thermal pad, which will help ease his aches and pains associated with the aging process. His movements will become slower; thus, it is so important to keep him active so as to enable him to keep his joints as supple as possible. This does not mean a lot of exercise one day and none the next. It is important to be consistent with your senior's exercise from day to day, week to week.

FEEDING THE SENIOR AKITA

Consider your Akita's diet at this stage as well. There is a commonly held belief that older

Bill Andrews photographed with Ch. Okii Yuki's Dragon House Ko-Go, the number-two dam of all time, at eleven years of age.

dogs need less protein. At least one of your authors disputes that, but both agree that older dogs need better food and usually a little less of it. As teeth wear down, bones may become a bit more difficult, but even the very old dog will treasure the fresh beef knucklebone. Chicken necks and wings, when given raw, are very soft and easily masticated.

We have been easily convinced about the special dietary needs of older dogs because it is true that they do seem to have less tolerance for commercially prepared foods. Rather than advise owners to switch to a more wholesome manner of feeding the dog, vets, advisors and dog-food companies suggest a "senior dog" diet. One would hope that there is a more holistic product in the "senior diet" bag or can, but owners can not always be sure.

If symptoms of food intolerance persist, it is up to the wise owner to identify and correct the real problem—the source and the type of food the dog is forced to consume. It is more than likely to be the chemicals and preservatives in prepared dog food to which the older dog has become sensitive. His immune system is not as strong as in years past and, just as with humans, his tolerance for some foods becomes lower with old age.

SIGNS OF AGING

An old dog starts to show one or more of the following symptoms:

- Sleep patterns are deeper and longer and the old dog is harder to awaken.
- Food intake diminishes.
- Responses to calls, whistles and other signals are ignored more and more.
- Eye contacts do not evoke tail wagging (assuming they once did).
- The hair on its face and paws starts to turn gray. The color breakdown usually starts around the eyes and mouth.

A classic example is the doctor who had a pet tortoise that he had kept since being in medical school. It was a quiet, trouble-free pet that safely could be hidden away. He had become very attached to the tortoise over their 20 years together. When the tortoise became ill, he took it to the vet. Nothing seemed to help and when it appeared that he might lose his relatively young (in tortoise years) friend, he located a zoological specialist who readily agreed to see them both.

The solution was so simple that it astounded the doctor. It changed the way he treated his patients and himself! As the body ages, dietary needs and preferences change. Whereas once we as youngsters could eat a whole pie every night, as adults we would look like hippos if we continued such wild indulgence. So we begin to at least think about "dieting" and eating more sensibly. As children, we probably didn't care that much for vegetables, but as middle-aged adults, they begin to have more appeal. Children, like puppies, demand huge energy reserves, obtained from large portions of calorie-rich foods. As adults, we need somewhat less high-energy foods, and if we continue to eat like children, we become obese. Adults may still enjoy a big juicy steak because, after all, we are omnivores, but we now accept veggies, even crave them, along with more fruit.

As mature adults, most humans eat both meat and vegetation—just like dogs and tortoises. But, as we approach old age, our food-processing equipment loses some of its ability, and, consequently, we begin to prefer foods that are less rich, easier to digest and quicker to eliminate. Dogs and other species realize that. Unlike humans, they don't watch television and read magazines that tout ever more wonderful culinary delights for the palette!

The zoo vet told the doctor to change the tortoise's diet and his 20-year-old friend would be just fine. With lifted eyebrow and a glance at the doctor's waistline, the vet suggested that it might be wise for the doctor also to heed the "prescription" given to his pet. He said to offer the tortoise more fresh green leafy vegetation and more fruits, while cutting back on the mealworms and packaged insects (meat protein) he had been feeding. It worked perfectly, and the doctor could almost hear his pet sigh with relief! Did the doctor change his own diet? We don't know—but I suspect, having reconsidered his medical teachings and applying his newfound knowledge and some common sense, that he lost a few pounds and became a healthier human.

Indeed your dog may develop digestive upset, malaise, arthritis,

Seniors tend to sleep away much of the day, though they still welcome the affections of their human families.

hot spots or skin rashes as he ages. But if you have been feeding only prepared foods, try giving him a little bit of rice or noodles. Then add a bit of cooked chicken or lamb from a healthy source, of course (not from a slaughter contaminated by hormones and antibiotics). Gradually shift him over to raw meat and bones. You may have to warm it slightly; don't expect him to gulp it down cold. As he learns what it is, he will try to open the freezer to get at it!

We cannot over-emphasize the importance of maintaining the healthy diet that your Akita has been used to throughout his life. As with all breeds, middle-aged to senior dogs have the tendency to gain weight. Obesity puts more stress on the body and can compound the problems already brought on by old age, so must be avoided for the dog's health. This can be controlled by balancing food intake, which might even require changing his food to a senior or "lite" diet, and being careful not to give too many treats.

Alternatively, as this breed can have a thyroid imbalance, have your veterinarian take a blood test for your Akita's thyroid level. Regular health checkups by your vet—twice annually—will help by identifying problems at an early stage. There are many products available for the elderly Akita, especially for the joints and mobility problems; these are available through your veterinarian or health food store.

WHAT TO LOOK FOR IN SENIORS

Most veterinarians and behaviorists use the seven-year mark as the time to consider an Akita a senior. The term "senior" does not imply that the dog is geriatric and has begun to fail in mind and body. Aging is essentially a slowing process. Humans readily admit that they feel a difference in their activity level from age 20 to 30, and then from 30 to 40, etc. By treating the seven-year-old dog as a senior, owners are able to implement certain therapeutic and preventative medical strategies with the help of their veterinarians. A senior-care program should include at least two veterinary visits per year, screening sessions to determine the dog's health status, as well as nutritional counseling. Veterinarians determine the senior dog's health status through a blood smear for a complete blood count, serum chemistry profile with electrolytes, urinalysis, blood pressure check, electrocardiogram, ocular tonometry (pressure on the eyeball) and dental prophylaxis.

Such an extensive program for senior dogs is well advised before owners start to see the obvious

HORMONAL PROBLEMS

Although graying is normal and expected in older dogs, a flaky coat or loss of hair is not. Such coat problems may point to a hormonal problem. Hypothyroidism, in which the thyroid gland fails to produce the normal amount of hormones, is one such problem. Your veterinarian can treat hypothyroidism with an oral supplement. The condition is more common in certain breeds, so discuss its likelihood in your dog with your breeder and vet.

physical signs of aging, such as slower and inhibited movement, graying, increased sleep/nap periods and disinterest in play and other activity. This preventative program promises a longer, healthier life for the aging dog. Among the physical problems common in aging dogs are the loss of sight and hearing, arthritis, kidney and liver failure, diabetes mellitus, heart disease and Cushing's disease (a hormonal disease).

In addition to the physical manifestations discussed, there are some behavioral changes and problems related to aging dogs. Dogs suffering from hearing or vision loss, dental discomfort or arthritis can become aggressive. Likewise the near-deaf and/or blind dog may be startled more easily and react in an unexpectedly aggressive manner. Seniors suffering from senility can become more impatient and irritable. Housesoiling accidents are associated with loss of mobility, kidney problems and loss of sphincter control, as well as plaque accumulation, physiological brain changes and reactions to medications. Older dogs, just like young puppies, suffer from separation anxiety, which can lead to excessive barking, whining, housesoiling and destructive behavior. Seniors may become fearful of everyday sounds, such as vacuum cleaners, heaters, thunder and passing traffic. Some dogs have difficulty sleeping, due to discomfort, the need for frequent toilet visits and the like.

Your dog, as he nears his twilight years, needs his owner's patience and good care more than ever. Never punish an older dog for an accident or abnormal behavior. Older dogs may not be able to remain crated for more than two or three hours. It may be time to give up a sofa or bed to your old friend. Although he may not seem as enthusiastic about your attention and petting, he does appreciate the considerations you offer as he gets older. Your Akita does not understand why his world is slowing down. Owners must make the transition into the golden years as pleasant and rewarding as possible.

Do Akitas make good show dogs? Both the authors agree, a resounding yes! Furthermore, both authors are breeder-exhibitors and cannot overstate the importance of showing dogs. The show ring is the proving ground of the whelping box. Unless a dog proves itself in the show ring, it does not earn a coveted place in a breeding program. Mrs. Andrews is

The Akita possesses a quiet dignity, a true quality that shines in the show ring.

certainly proud of her records in the show ring, as she was the first breeder-exhibitor to handle an Akita to a Group placement, not to mention the first to handle an Akita to multiple Bests in Show. Both authors have bred champions, and Mrs. Andrews holds the record for breeding more American champions than any other breeder—if fact, more than even any two kennels combined. Mrs. Carpenter is an exhibitor as well as an international judge.

So, yes, the Akita makes a fabulous show dog, though he'll never be as showy as a Standard Poodle or as cocky as a Shih Tzu. The Akita, with his quiet dignity and natural beauty, knows he is special and knows he has no equals. That is the essence of *Akita*, and that is the essence of a winning show dog.

When you purchase your Akita, you will make it clear to the breeder whether you want one just as a proud companion and pet, or if you hope to be buying an Akita with show prospects. No reputable breeder will sell you a young puppy and tell you that it is *definitely* of show quality, for so

American-style Akitas are popular around the world, and often win in the show ring. This dog is titling at a South American show.

much can go wrong during the early months of a puppy's development. If you plan to show, what you will hopefully have acquired is a puppy with "show potential."

To the novice, exhibiting an Akita in the show ring may look easy, but it takes a lot of hard work and devotion to do top winning at a show such as the prestigious Westminster Kennel Club dog show, not to mention a little luck, too!

The first concept that the canine novice learns when watching a dog show is that each dog first competes against members of his own breed. Once the judge has selected the best member of each breed (Best of Breed), provided

that the show is judged on a Group system, that chosen dog will compete with other dogs in his group. Finally, the dogs chosen first in each group will compete for Best in Show.

The second concept that you must understand is that the dogs are not actually compared against one another. The judge compares

AKC GROUPS

For showing purposes, the American Kennel Club divides its recognized breeds into seven groups: Sporting Dogs, Hounds, Working Dogs, Terriers, Toys, Non-Sporting Dogs and Herding Dogs.

With practice, your Akita will respond to your subtlest commands in the show ring. Standing still at attention, waiting for a tiny taste of bait, this Akita awaits her handler's next command.

each dog against his breed standard, the written description of the ideal specimen that is approved by the American Kennel Club (AKC). While some early breed standards were indeed based on specific dogs that were famous or popular, many dedicated enthusiasts say that a perfect specimen, as described in the standard, has never walked into a show ring, has never been bred and, to the woe of dog breeders around the globe, does not exist. Breeders attempt to get as

INFORMATION ON CLUBS

You can get information about dog shows from the national kennel clubs:

American Kennel Club
5580 Centerview Dr., Raleigh, NC 27606-3390
www.akc.org

United Kennel Club
100 E. Kilgore Road, Kalamazoo, MI 49002
www.ukcdogs.com

Canadian Kennel Club
89 Skyway Ave., Suite 100, Etobicoke, Ontario
M9W 6R4 Canada
www.ckc.ca

The Kennel Club
1-5 Clarges St., Piccadilly, London W1Y 8AB, UK
www.the-kennel-club.org.uk

Fédération Cynologique Internationale
14, rue Leopold II, B-6530 Thuin, Belgium
www.fci.be

close to this ideal as possible with every litter, but theoretically the "perfect" dog is so elusive that it is impossible.

If you are interested in exploring the world of dog showing, your best bet is to join your local breed club or the national parent club, which is the Akita Club of America. These clubs often host both regional and national specialties, shows only for Akitas, which can include conformation as well as obedience and agility trials. Even if you have no intention of competing with your Akita, a specialty is like a festival for lovers of the breed who congregate to share their favorite

topic: Akitas! Clubs also send out newsletters, and some organize training days and seminars in order that people may learn more about their chosen breed. To locate the breed club closest to you, contact the American Kennel Club, which furnishes the rules and regulations for all of these events plus general dog registration and other basic requirements of dog ownership.

The American Kennel Club offers three kinds of conformation shows: An all-breed show (for all AKC-recognized breeds), a specialty show (for one breed only, usually sponsored by the parent club) and a Group show (for all breeds in the group). The Akita competes in the Working Group.

For a dog to become an AKC champion of record, the dog must accumulate 15 points at the shows from at least three different judges, including two "majors." A "major" is defined as a three-, four- or five-point win, and the number of points per win is determined by the number of dogs entered in the show on that day. Depending on the breed, the number of points that are awarded varies. More dogs are needed to rack up the points in more popular breeds, and fewer dogs are needed in less popular breeds.

Author Meg Purnell-Carpenter awards her choice for Best in Specialty Show at an FCI show in Japan. What an honor for an English breeder-judge to be invited to Japan to judge the Akita!

At any dog show, only one dog and one bitch of each breed can win points. Dog showing does not offer "co-ed" classes. Dogs and bitches never compete against each other in the classes. Non-champion dogs are called "class dogs" because they compete in one of five classes. Dogs are entered in a particular class depending on age and previous show wins. To begin, there is the Puppy Class (for 6- to 9-month-olds and for 9- to 12-month-olds); this class is followed by the Novice Class (for dogs that have not won any first prizes except in the Puppy Class or three first prizes in the Novice Class and have not accumulated any points toward their champion title); the Bred-by-Exhibitor Class (for dogs handled by their breeders or by one of the breeder's immediate family); the American-bred Class (for dogs bred in the US); and the Open Class (for any dog that is not a champion).

The judge at the show begins judging the Puppy Class, first dogs and then bitches, and proceeds through the classes. The judge places his winners first through fourth in each class. In the Winners Class, the first-place winners of each class compete with one another to determine Winners Dog and Winners Bitch. The judge also places a Reserve Winners Dog and Reserve Winners Bitch, which could be awarded the points in the case of a disqualification. The Winners Dog and Winners Bitch—the two that are awarded the points for the breed—then compete with any champions of record (often called "specials") entered in the show. The judge reviews the Winners Dog, Winners Bitch and all of the champions to select his Best of Breed. The Best of Winners is selected between the Winners Dog and Winners Bitch. Were one of these two to be selected Best of Breed, it would automatically be named Best of Winners as well. Finally the judge selects his Best of Opposite Sex to the Best of Breed winner.

Black-masked fawn Akita, taking home the spoils at a dog show!

A lovely pinto Akita, posing with her handler at an outdoor conformation show.

At a Group show or all-breed show, the Best of Breed winners from each breed then compete against one another for Group One through Group Four. The judge compares each Best of Breed to his breed standard, and the dog that most closely lives up to the ideal for his breed is selected as Group One. Finally, all seven group winners (from the Sporting Group, Working Group, Hound Group, etc.) compete for Best in Show.

To find out about dog shows in your area, you can subscribe to the American Kennel Club's monthly magazine, the *American Kennel Gazette* and the accompanying *Events Calendar*. You can also look in your local newspaper for advertisements for dog shows in your area or go on the Internet to the AKC's website, http:www.akc.org.

If your Akita is six months of age or older and registered with the AKC, you can enter him in a dog show where the breed is offered classes. Provided that your Akita does not have a disqualifying fault, he can compete. Only unaltered dogs can be entered in a dog show, so if you have spayed or neutered your Akita, your dog cannot compete in conformation shows. Altered dogs, however, can participate in other AKC events such as obedience trials and the Canine Good Citizen program.

Before you actually step into the ring, you would be well

NEATNESS COUNTS
Surely you've spent hours grooming your dog to perfection for the show ring, but don't forget about yourself! While the dog should be the center of attention, it is important that you also appear neat and clean. Wear smart, appropriate clothes and comfortable shoes in a color that contrasts with your dog's coat. Look and act like a professional.

advised to sit back and observe the judge's ring procedure. The judge asks each handler to "stack" the dog, hopefully showing the dog off to his best advantage. The judge will observe the dog from a distance and from different angles, and approach the dog to check his teeth, overall structure, alertness and muscle tone, as well as consider how well the dog "conforms" to the standard. Most importantly, the judge will have the exhibitor move the dog around the ring in some pattern that he should specify. Finally, the judge will give the dog one last look before moving on to the next exhibitor.

If you are not in the top four in your class at your first show, do not be discouraged. Be patient and consistent, and you may eventually find yourself in a winning line-up. Remember that the winners were once in your shoes and have devoted many hours and much money to earn the placement. If you find that your dog is losing every time and never getting a nod, it may be time to consider a different dog sport or to just enjoy your Akita as a pet. Parent clubs offer other events, such as agility, obedience, instinct tests and more, which may be of interest to the owner of a well-trained Akita.

OBEDIENCE TRIALS

Obedience trials in the US trace back to the early 1930s when organized obedience training was developed to demonstrate how well dog and owner could work together. The pioneer of obedience trials is Mrs. Helen Whitehouse Walker, a Standard Poodle fancier, who designed a series of exercises after the Associated Sheep, Police Army Dog Society of Great Britain. Since the days of Mrs. Walker, obedience trials have grown by leaps and bounds, and today

there are over 2,000 trials held in the US every year, with more than 100,000 dogs competing. Any AKC-registered dog can enter an obedience trial, regardless of conformational disqualifications or neutering.

AGILITY TRIALS

Having had its origins in the UK back in 1977, AKC agility had its official beginning in August 1994, when the first licensed agility trials were held. The AKC allows all registered breeds (including Miscellaneous Class breeds) to participate, providing the dog is 12 months of age or older.

Agility is designed so that the handler demonstrates how well the dog can work at his side. The handler directs his dog over an obstacle course that includes jumps as well as tires, the dog walk, weave poles, pipe tunnels, collapsed tunnels, etc. While working his way through the course, the dog must keep one eye and ear on the handler and the rest of his body on the course. The handler gives verbal and hand signals to guide the dog through the course. Agility is great fun for dog and owner with many rewards for everyone involved. Interested owners should join a training club that has obstacles and experienced agility handlers who can introduce you and your Akita to the "ropes" (and tires, tunnels, etc.).

TEMPERAMENT PLUS

Although it seems that physical conformation is the only factor considered in the show ring, temperament is also of utmost importance. An aggressive or fearful dog should not be shown, as bad behavior will not be tolerated and may pose a threat to the judge, other exhibitors, you and your dog.

INDEX

Page numbers in **boldface** indicate illustrations.

My Akita

PUT YOUR PUPPY'S FIRST PICTURE HERE

Dog's Name _____

Date _____ Photographer _____